Off the Beaten Track

Epigraphy at the Borders

Proceedings of the VI EAGLE
International Meeting
(24-25 September 2015, Bari, Italy)

Edited by

A. E. Felle
A. Rocco

Archaeopress Archaeology

Archaeopress Publishing Ltd
Gordon House
276 Banbury Road
Oxford OX2 7ED

www.archaeopress.com

ISBN 978 1 78491 322 9
ISBN 978 1 78491 323 6 (e-Pdf)

© Archaeopress and the individual authors 2016

Front cover design by Maria Martinelli (with EAGLE Project image by Luca Giberti)

The editing of this volume was funded by
Europeana EAGLE Project - Europeana network of Ancient Greek and Latin Epigraphy
(CIP - Competitiveness and Innovation framework Programme 2007-2013, Best Practice Network
[Grant Agreement no. 325122])

All rights reserved. No part of this book may be reproduced, stored in retrieval system,
or transmitted, in any form or by any means, electronic, mechanical, photocopying or otherwise,
without the prior written permission of the copyright owners.

Printed in England by Oxuniprint, Oxford

This book is available direct from Archaeopress or from our website www.archaeopress.com

VI EAGLE International Event
Dipartimento di Scienze dell'Antichità e del Tardoantico
University of Bari "Aldo Moro" - Italy
24-25 September 2015

PROGRAMME

Welcome

P. Totaro - Director of the Department of Classics and Late Antiquity - University of Bari "Aldo Moro"
S. Orlandi - EAGLE Coordinator
C. Carletti - Epigraphic Database Bari (EDB) Creator

EAGLE Portal and Mobile App Official Launch

C. Prandoni - Promoter Srl, Pisa
How to search inscriptions

P. Liuzzo - University of Heidelberg
Vocabularies, Translations, Bibliographies

Ph. Martineau - Eureva, Paris
Eagle Flagship Mobile Application

EAGLE Featured Stories

M. Šašel Kos - Research Centre of the Slovenian Academy of Sciences and Arts Institute of Archaeology, Ljubljana
The Disappearing Tombstone and Other Stories from **Emona**

F. Mambrini, W. Schmidle - German Archaeological Institute, Berlin
The EAGLE Storytelling Application
How to feature your story on the EAGLE Storytelling App - Hands On

---

Off the Beaten Track. Epigraphy at the Borders

A.E. Felle - University of Bari "Aldo Moro"
Off the Beaten Track. An Introduction

G. Sarullo - "Kore" University, Enna
Inscriptiones Latinae Antiquissimae: the Encoding Challenge of the ILA Project

R. Benefiel, H. Sypniewski - Washington and Lee University, Millsaps College
Working with texts and images: The Graffiti of Herculaneum

A. De Santis, I. Rossi - Scuola Normale Superiore, Pisa
Is still Arabia at the margins of digital epigraphy? Challenges in the digitization of the pre-Islamic inscriptions in the project DASI

A. Rocco - University of Bari "Aldo Moro"
From officina lapidaria *to D.I.Y: encoding inscriptions from the Roman Catacombs*

A. Rhoby - Austrian Academy of Sciences, Vienna
Challenges of Byzantine Epigraphy in the 21st Century

L. Cacchioli, N. Cannata, A. Tiburzi - Sapienza, University of Rome
EDV - Italian Medieval Epigraphy in the Vernacular (IX-XV c.): a new database

H. Cornwell, J. Massèglia - University of Oxford
Signs, Symbols and Spaces in the Ashmolean Latin Collection

J. Remesal - University of Barcelona
Amphorae epigraphy, formally represented epigraphy

D. Malerba - University of Bari "Aldo Moro"
Data Science for Historical Inquiries

P. Liuzzo - University of Heidelberg
Conclusions

Contents

Foreword 1
Silvia Orlandi
Content 1
Chronology 2
Geography 2
Dissemination 3

Off the Beaten Track. Epigraphy at the Borders. An Introduction 5
Antonio Enrico Felle
Bibliography 13

The Encoding Challenge of the ILA Project 15
Giulia Sarullo
Direction of writing 16
Orientation of the letters 22
Conclusion 25
Bibliography 25

Images and Text on the Walls of Herculaneum:
Designing the Ancient Graffiti Project 29
Rebecca R. Benefiel and Holly M. Sypniewski
Our Material 31
Documenting extant figural graffiti 36
Building the Ancient Graffiti Project Search Engine 45
Bibliography 48

Is still Arabia at the margins of digital Epigraphy? Challenges in the
digitization of the pre-Islamic inscriptions in the project DASI 49
Alessandra Avanzini, Annamaria De Santis, Daniele Marotta and Irene Rossi
DASI: overview of the project 49
Ancient South Arabian epigraphy: introduction to the subject 51
A step forward from CSAI: semi-structured or structured information? ... 52
Text encoding: the alignment to a standard 52
Exposing the EpiDoc files 57
DASI Lexicon for linguistic study 60
Bibliography 62

From *Officina Lapidaria* to D.I.Y. Encoding inscriptions from the Christian Roman Catacombs 63
Anita Rocco
Vocabularies 74
Multilingual inscriptions 76
'Aberrant' forms 77
Direction and orientation of the text 78
Text and Images.. 80
Bibliography 82

Challenges of Byzantine Epigraphy in the 21st Century. A Short Note........... 85
Andreas Rhoby
Bibliography.. 90

EDV. Italian Medieval Epigraphy in the Vernacular (9th-15th century). A new Database 91
Luna Cacchioli, Nadia Cannata and Alessandra Tiburzi
Introduction.. 91
The nature of the database 93
Oral voices and literary languages. A few considerations 93
Classifying the materials... 95
Linguistic Variety 106
Issues in the digitiization of epigraphic material... 111
The Database template 122
Bibliography.. 126

Signals, Symbols, and Spaces in the Ashmolean Latin Collection 131
Hannah Cornwell and Jane Masséglia
The Rationale behind the AshLI project 131
The Nature of the Corpus 131
Applying EpiDoc to the AshLI Corpus. 132
The Gaia mark 133
Form and appearance of the text... 135
Execution techniques 136
Direction of the text 137

Epigraphy out there 141
Pietro Liuzzo
Editing epigraphic texts 143
Vocabularies 147
The landscape of digital epigraphy.. 148
Sustainability and Conclusions 153
Bibliography.. 154

List of Figures and Tables

***A.E. Felle*: Off the Beaten Track. Epigraphy at the Borders An Introduction**
Figure 1. Results by searching the string 'refriger*' in form of KWIC list (screenshot from the very first database about ICVR, Bari 1989: image Dipartimento di Studi Umanistici, University of Bari 'Aldo Moro'). 6
Figure 2. Beth She'arim (Israel). Epitaph of Daniel, from Tyre, with menorah with final acclamation in Hebrew shalom. 4th cent. (from Schwabe and Lifshitz 1974, n. 149) 6
Figure 3. EDB16838 (http://www.edb.uniba.it/epigraph/16838). End of 4th cent. AD (image Epigraphic Database Bari). 7
Figure 4. Monte Sant'Angelo (Gargano, Northern Apulia, Italy). Graffiti on the rock in the Sacred Cave of st.Michael. 7th - 8 cent. AD (image Dipartimento di Studi Umanistici, University of Bari 'Aldo Moro'). 9
Figure 5. Rome, via Ardeatina, catacomb of Domitilla. Graffito in cursive writing. ICVR, III 8034; EDB24880. First half of 4th cent. AD (image Epigraphic Database Bari and Papal Commission of Sacred Archaeology) 10
Figure 6. Rome, via Ardeatina, catacomb of Domitilla. ICVR, III 7306; EDB24027. End of 3rd cent. AD (image Epigraphic Database Bari and Papal Commission of Sacred Archaeology) ... 11
Figure 7. Trani (Apulia, Italy), Cathedral. Images and texts scratched on a funerary limestone slab (from Carletti 1988). 7th - 8th cent. AD (image Dipartimento di Studi Umanistici, University of Bari 'Aldo Moro'). 11

***G. Sarullo*: The Encoding Challenge of the ILA Project**
Figure 1. The Forum inscription, side B and C (apograph by Comparetti 1900 elaborated by the Author) 18
Figure 2. Unicode characters representing the upside-down directions of writing. 18
Figure 3. The lamina from Lavinium (apograph by G. Sarullo). 19
Figure 4. The Tibur pedestal inscription (apograph by Mancini 1979) 19
Figure 5. Inscription from the cemetery of Commodilla in Rome , ICVR, II, 6117 - EDB19242 (from Rocco 2005: 296). 20
Figure 6. Unicode characters representing rotated directions of writing 21
Figure 7. Other suitable Unicode characters not available in all the directions needed. 21
Figure 8. Partial markup of the inscription on the lamina from Lavinium. 22
Figure 9. Partial markup of the Tibur pedestal inscription. 22
Figure 10. Detail of CIL, I2 1799 (EDR147038), elaborated by the Author (from CIL: tav. 84, no. 3). ... 23
Figure 11. The Tibur pedestal inscription (photograph by Marta Muscariello, elaborated by the Author in order to highlight reversed and upside-down letters). 24

***R.R. Benefiel and H.M. Sypniewski*: Images and Text on the Walls of Herculaneum: Designing the Ancient Graffiti Project**
Figure 1. Graffito of gladiators from Pompeii (CIL, IV 8055a and 8055b) 30
Figure 2. Drawing of a gladiator, mentioned at CIL, IV 1481a (from Garrucci 1856, Tab. XV 6) 30
Figure 3. A scene depicting a gladiatorial event, sketched on a tomb outside the Porta Nocera at Pompeii (CIL, IV 10237) 31
Figure 4. The entries of CIL, IV 2315-2316 and 2319, representing figural graffiti via brief description in italics 32
Figure 5. Line-drawing depicting both text and image from Herculaneum (CIL, IV 10493) 33
Figure 6. CIL entry for an alphabetic series, which appeared near figural graffiti (CIL, IV 10711). 34
Figure 7. CIL entry for the name Onesimus, with numerous figural graffiti described in the apparatus (CIL, IV 10561) 35
Figure 8. Line-drawing displaying a collection of textual and figural graffiti (CIL, IV 8383-8386); unpublished sketch of Matteo Della Corte from the archives of the Corpus Inscriptionum Latinarum at the Berlin-Brandenburg Academy of Science and Humanities 37
Figure 9. EDR143634. EDR entry for gladiatorial helmet in the Casa del Gran Portale at Herculaneum, with nearby helmets associated via hyperlinks 38

Figure 10. Example of an entry for a figural graffito not found in CIL (EDR144514)...................... 40
Figure 11. Figural graffito from Herculaneum (from Langner 2001: n. 1372) 41
Figure 12. CIL entry for textual and figural graffiti (CIL, IV 8185) 42
Figure 13. CIL, IV 10676, with figural graffito noted 43
Figure 14. Apograph of figural graffito referred to in the note at CIL, IV 10676 (from Langner 2001: n. 309) 43
Figure 15. EDR143636, with description of figural graffito (a head) interpreted variously 44
Figure 16. Launch pad of The Ancient Graffiti Project Search Engine 45
Figure 17. Figural graffiti results, only from Herculaneum 46
Figure 18. AGP Drawing Category options for retrieving figural graffiti 47

A. Avanzini, A. De Santis, D. Marotta and I. Rossi: Is still Arabia at the margins of digital Epigraphy? Challenges in the digitization of the pre-Islamic inscriptions in the project DASI

Figure 1. Minaic inscription MṢM 3645 from the Military Museum of Ṣanʿāʾ (image DASI by permission of General Organization of Antiquities and Museums, Yemen)............................. 50
Figure 2. Editor of the 'Epigraph' with example of text encoding. 54
Figure 3. Representation of the editorial interventions in DASI and in the main systems of representation envisaged by EpiDoc. 55
Figure 4. Onomastic elements and related tags used by DASI. 56
Figure 5. Textual portions and related tags used by DASI. 59
Figure 6. Lexicon of the Minaic corpus: entities and their relations. 61

A. Rocco: From *Officina Lapidaria* to D.I.Y: encoding inscriptions from the Christian Roman Catacombs

Figure 1. Plan of the Roman theatre of Ostia (from Buonopane 2012: 202) and transcriptions of the probable writing tests (from CIL XIV).. 64
Figure 2. Workshop Signs from Rome: CIL, VI 9556 (from Di Stefano Manzella 1987: 248), 9557 and EDR126742 (from Manacorda 2000: 290-291) and Palermo: CIL, X 7296 (from Carletti 2015: 358). ... 65
Figure 3. A stonecutter at work (drawing: Velia Polito). 67
Figure 4. Reused occasional supports: EDB21639 and EDB32737 (from Epigraphic Database Bari). .. 68
Figure 5. Multiple texts on the same support: EDB21490/EDB39651 and EDB39650 (from Epigraphic Database Bari). 69
Figure 6. Asimmetrical and irregolar disposition of text and images on the inscribed field: EDB34691; EDB21490; EDB33608 and EDB41548 (from Epigraphic Database Bari). 70
Figure 7. Examples of 'a cordone' shape incision: EDB18703 and EDB34915 (from Epigraphic Database Bari).... 70
Figure 8. Insertion of cursive, minuscule and uncial element in capital based inscriptions: EDB31855; EDB3384; EDB33627 and EDB37051 (from Epigraphic Database Bari). 71
Figure 9. The variety of executing technique: EDB22522; EDB15426; EDB24678 and EDB16094 (from Epigraphic Database Bari). 72
Figure 10. Painted inscriptions on marble and brickwork: EDB16027 and EDB18301 (from Epigraphic Database Bari). 73
Figure 11. Inscription 'a nastro' traced on the mortar: EDB19359 (from Epigraphic Database Bari).... 74
Figure 12. Controlled vocabularies for Type of support, Executing technique and Function fields. 75
Figure 13. Iscription engraved and painted: EDB15301 (from Epigraphic Database Bari)............. 75
Figure 14. Cohexistence of Greek and Latin elements: EDB6231; EDB12309 and EDB13539 (from Epigraphic Database Bari). 76
Figure 15. Dealing with so-called 'aberrant' forms (EDB18067, from Epigraphic Database Bari)..... 77
Figure 16. 'A nastro' inscription (EDB22869/EDB22870) with transcription (from Epigraphic Database Bari). 78
Figure 17. Unicode characters representing directions and orientation of writing...................... 79
Figure 18. Transcription of EDB22869/EDB22870 according to the solutions proposed. 79
Figure 19. Interactions between text and images: EDB18809, EDB9652 and EDB32412 (from Epigraphic Database Bari). 80
Figure 20. Transcriptions of EDB6444 (ICVR VIII 21163) (from Epigraphic Database Bari)............ 80
Figure 21. Images in the middle of the text: EDB29046; EDB19068; EDB32108 and text inside the image: EDB31546 (from Epigraphic Database Bari). 81

***L. Cacchioli, N. Cannata and A. Tiburzi*: EDV Italian Medieval Epigraphy in the Vernacular (9th-15th century). A new Database**
Figure 1. The distribution of the material. 92
Figure 2. Venice, Campo Sant'Angelo, Inscription of Fanciulli della Pietà (half 14th century)....... 97
Figure 3. Rome, Church of S. Cecilia, Inscription of Oddariello Boccazzola (14th century) 98
Figure 4. Modena, Museo Lapidario Estense, Inscription of Francesco Roncaglia (1396)............. 99
Figure 5. Bologna, Bologna, Museo Civico Medievale, Tombstone of knight Filippo Desideri (1315).. 100
Figure 6. Bologna, Bologna, Museo Civico Medievale, Tombstone of knight Filippo Desideri (1315) – particular. 101
Figure 7. Civita Castellana, Church of S. Antonio, Cariatide (12th century)................... 102
Figure 8. Civita Castellana, Church of S. Antonio, Cariatide and Telamone (12th century) 102
Figure 9. Venice, exterior wall of the Tesoro della Basilica di San Marco, Bench in San Marco (late 14th century) 103
Figure 10. Rome, Church of S. Maria in Trastevere, Inscription of Anello detto Tortora (beginning of 15th century) 110
Figure 11. Subiaco, Sacro Speco, Fresco of Scala Santa with Trionfo della Morte (14th century) 112
Figure 12. Subiaco, Sacro Speco, Fresco of Scala Santa with Trionfo della Morte (14th century) – particular 1. 113
Figure 13. Subiaco, Sacro Speco, Fresco of Scala Santa with Trionfo della Morte (14th century) – particular 2. 113
Figure 14. Poggio Mirteto, Church of S. Paolo, Incontro dei vivi e dei morti (14th century)....... 114
Figure 15. Poggio Mirteto, Church of S. Paolo, Incontro dei vivi e dei morti (14th century) – particular 1. 115
Figure 16. Foligno, Palazzo Trinci. Museo della città, Loggia di Romolo e Remo, Stories of Romulus and Remus (1411-1412). 119
Figure 17. Foligno, Palazzo Trinci. Museo della città, Loggia di Romolo e Remo, Stories of Romulus and Remus (1411-1412) - particular. 120

***H. Cornwell and J. Masséglia*: Signals, Symbols, and Spaces in the Ashmolean Latin Collection**
Figure 1. The Odda Stone (AN1896-1908 M.300), an 11th century inscription originally from Gloucestershire, England. An unusual feature of the inscription is that certain letters are inscribed within a preceeding letter (image: Ashmolean Latin Inscriptions Project)............ 135
Figure 2. Top row, left to right: gemstone (AN1890.247) engraved with a crab and retrograde letters; brickstamp (ANTN1864) with retrograde letters; bottom: fragmentary terra sigillata mould (AN1889.14c) with retrograde letters (images: Ashmolean Latin Inscriptions Project).. 138
Figure 3. First century AD brickstamp (AN1872.1527) with direction of text in semi-circle and left to right, and an erasure in the second line (image: Ashmolean Latin Inscriptions Project).. 139
Figure 4: Votive altar from South Shields, England (ANChandler 3.3), dedicated on behalf of Caracalla and Geta. Geta's name has been erased in lines 7-8 (image: Ashmolean Latin Inscriptions Project). 140

***P. Liuzzo*: Epigraphy out there**
Figure 1. Digitized Cultural Heritage in Europe (from http://strategy2020.europeana.eu by Elco van Staveneren) 150

Foreword

Silvia Orlandi
EAGLE Project Scientific Coordinator - 'Sapienza' University of Rome

Since the beginning, and in response to a real need of the academic community, the main aim of the EAGLE project has been 'to make accessible texts and images - with the related metadata - of a high percentage of the ancient Greek and Latin inscriptions dating from the seventh century BC to the seventh century AD'. Thanks to a huge job of harmonization and disambiguation of data coming from different content providers, we can say that the project is going to accomplish this mission.

But since the beginning, we have all been aware that the fulfilment of this task wouldn't satisfy all the needs of epigraphic research or answer the questions. Just the opposite: as the work proceeds, we always find new problems, but also new issues, and patterns that could be followed.

As scientific supervisor, I don't think that this is a negative aspect of the project, but rather proof that we are probably going in the right direction. This explains the wide variety of themes discussed during the First EAGLE International Conference in 2014 in Paris, the dramatic growth of networking activities in many, often unexpected directions, and the interest for the EAGLE project shown by colleagues and institutions dealing with epigraphic materials belonging to different cultures and civilizations.

All this has led us to consider the possibility, and therefore the need, to discuss problems that go beyond the 'official', original limits of the EAGLE projects in many different ways: problems regarding content, chronology, geographic areas, and forms of communication.

Content

The EAGLE project has a very strong thematic character, focused as it is on ancient Greek and Roman epigraphy. However, the inscriptions are never considered as mere texts, but rather as inscribed monuments, where archaeological and topographical aspects has the same importance as the textual content. In this framework, images have a fundamental role, of which the importance and implications are becoming clearer and clearer. Palaeographic analysis of inscriptions, for example, can benefit greatly from a 'visual' approach and from the technical possibilities opened up by the inclusion of image-based search included in the EAGLE portal. In the same way, special attention should be paid to images that are strictly connected to the epigraphic texts in many graffiti and Christian inscriptions, where the drawings play a key role in communicating the epigraphic message: they have to be encoded in a digital archive in order to keep their close connection with the texts and, at the same time, their specific nature.

Chronology

The first examples of Greek and Latin inscriptions date from the end of the eighth - beginning of the seventh century BC. While there is no agreement among the scholars about the beginning of Medieval epigraphy, the eighth century AD seems to be a turning point in epigraphic habit. The chronological range chosen for the EAGLE project is therefore a convention that doesn't exclude the importance of materials coming from a more remote past, on the one side, or belonging to the Middle Ages, on the other. In both cases, an accurate reflection is needed: archaic texts often present palaeographic characters, writing techniques and linguistic issues that are completely different from those found in classical inscriptions; Byzantine epigraphy, compared to ancient Greek epigraphic materials, shows interesting differences in form and content; inscriptions written in Italian *volgare*, abandoning the use of classical Latin, share nevertheless a surprising number of technical aspects with ancient epigraphs. All these examples, which sometimes cross the chronological borders of the EAGLE project, give an important contribution to the epigraphic science not only by widening the variety texts, artifacts and languages considered, but above all giving epigraphers new eyes to look at traditional problems, and new ways to find unexpected connections.

Geography

The Mediterranean world, the traditional enviroment of the Greek and Latin civilizations, is the geographic focus of the EAGLE project. But since the beginning projects dealing with epigraphy of different areas have expressed their interest in sharing knowledge and experiences. After all, contacts with the Arabian peninsula, the Indian Ocean and the far East are well-documented in Roman times, and interesting challenges and considerations can come from the knowledge of completely different epigraphies, showing first of all the incredibly widespread use of this form of communication. Everywhere in the world, in all time periods, men have chosen to abandon the traditional, daily way of writing to make what can be called an 'inscription', often sharing the same needs, feelings or hopes. And this consideration is of invaluable help in dealing with all kinds of epigraphic material, no matter where it comes from.

Dissemination

Greek and Latin inscriptions are often difficult to understand, not only because they are written in ancient languages and alphabets, but also because they are sometimes communicated and explained only in 'academic' publications, intended for a public of scholars and learned people. Crossing the borders of classical epigraphy also means going beyond the limits of the traditional way of presenting ancient inscriptions, opening the knowledge of these texts to a broader public. The EAGLE mobile application, using a well-tested form of image-based recognition system, and the EAGLE storytelling application, which underlines the narrative content included in every inscription, even in the most apparently simple text, are here in University of Bari officially presented for the first time. Thanks to, in the one case, a technology that allows for the identification of an inscription without digitising any text, and, in the other, the thousands of beautiful and interesting stories that can be told starting from an inscription, we hope to find a new, innovative way to reach a broader public, ready to share with us the persuasion that even epigraphy ... can be fun.

In other words, exploring roads that are - in many different ways - 'off the beaten track' doesn't mean betraying the original spirit of the EAGLE project, but, on the contrary, improving our knowledge of ancient inscriptions and of the world that produced them, sharing this knowledge within a wide network of best practices, and making it accessible in both traditional and innovative ways.

Off the Beaten Track. Epigraphy at the Borders
An Introduction

Antonio Enrico Felle
Epigraphic Database Bari – University of Bari 'Aldo Moro'

Usually, the introductions are expected to be boring and often are considered useless... So, I wrote very few words only to describe the agenda of our meeting and to try to explain - I hope - its *raison d'être*.
First of all, I draw your attention to the content of the text published on *Current Epigraphy* on 25th May 2015 which describes our conference:[1]

> 'Hosted by EAGLE (Europeana network of Ancient Greek and Latin Epigraphy), [the Meeting] is the sixth in a series of international events planned by this European and international consortium with the support of the Department of Classics and Late Antiquity Studies at the University of Bari "Aldo Moro".
>
> The aim of this initiative is to create a shared space to discuss the issues addressed in digitizing inscriptions characterised by unusual features in comparison to the usual epigraphic habit.'

The keyword of our meeting is the adjective "unusual".
Since the late Eighties, at the outset of the database of the ancient Christian inscriptions from Rome, Carlo Carletti (the creator of the current Epigraphic Database Bari, now EDB[2]) and I came face to face with many *unusual* inscriptions, from different perspectives, in relation to the so-called "normal" ancient inscriptions.

I will try to explain it with an example (Figure 1).
As we can see, we had some troubles processing recurrent Christian inscriptions in which images, symbols, or generally non-alphabetical signs play a very special and important role in connection - or not - with texts or, also, with some single letters.

This odd feature of ancient Christian inscriptions is commonly explained supposing that these inscriptions were commissioned by non-alphabetized patrons to non-professional stone-cutters, but the issue is not so simple: moreover, we see

---

[1] http://www.currentepigraphy.org/2015/05/25/epigraphy-at-borders-bari/.
[2] http://www.edb.uniba.it.

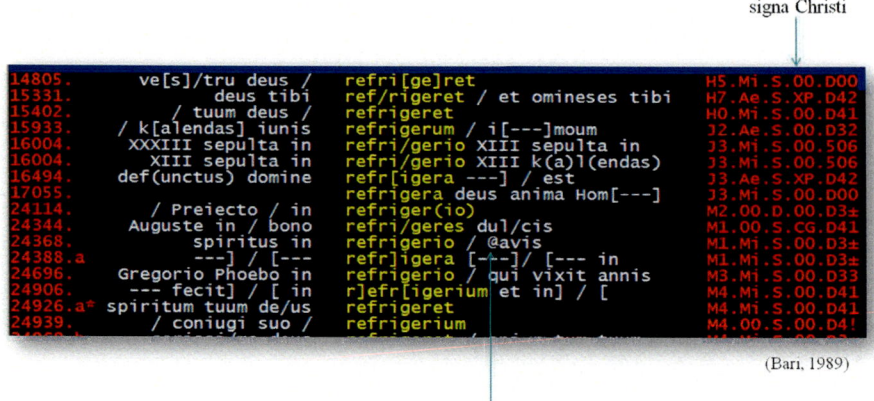

FIGURE 1. RESULTS BY SEARCHING THE STRING 'REFRIGER*' IN FORM OF KWIC LIST (SCREENSHOT FROM THE VERY FIRST DATABASE ABOUT ICVR, BARI 1989: IMAGE DIPARTIMENTO DI STUDI UMANISTICI, UNIVERSITY OF BARI 'ALDO MORO').

the same phenomenon also in contemporary Jewish inscriptions (Figure 2): it has evidently other reasons.

Today we still have trouble processing these documents in EDB, because the various relationships between texts and images (positioning, relative chronology, prevalence, mutual significance) are not encoded yet by current conventions and transcribing systems (even in EpiDoc). We can inform about the existence of these images only giving a short description in Latin, between double parenthesis: but, nothing about their positioning and their relation to the letters (Figure 3).

This is not an issue relating only to the Late Antique Christian - or also Jewish - inscriptions. Our experience with the

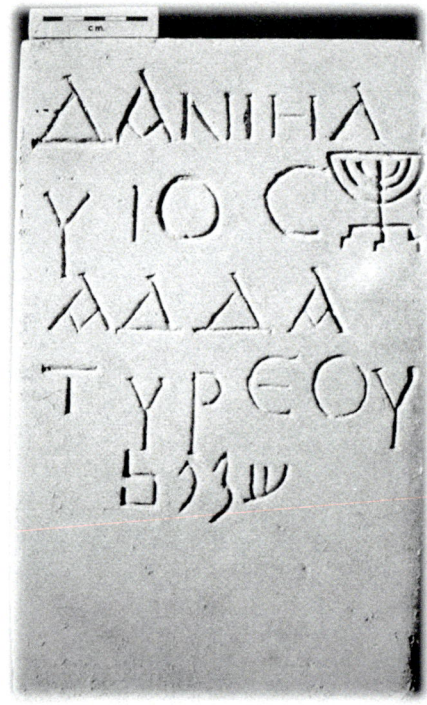

FIGURE 2. BETH SHE'ARIM (ISRAEL). EPITAPH OF DANIEL, FROM TYRE, WITH MENORAH WITH FINAL ACCLAMATION IN HEBREW SHALOM. 4TH CENT. (FROM SCHWABE AND LIFSHITZ 1974, N. 149).

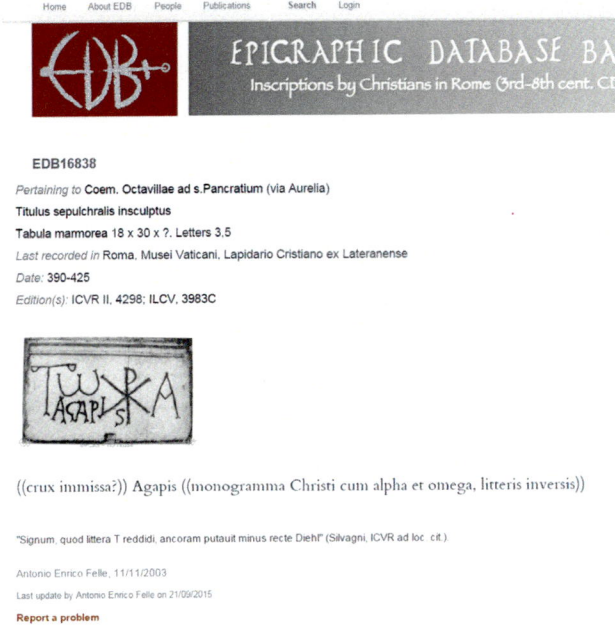

FIGURE 3. EDB16838 (HTTP://WWW.EDB.UNIBA.IT/EPIGRAPH/16838). END OF 4TH CENT. AD (IMAGE EPIGRAPHIC DATABASE BARI).

Epigraphic Database Bari - and with other databases - is probably the same as that of other scholars involved in similar projects. I believe that the issues presented here, in our 'shared space', can be approached thanks to the simultaneous attendance of specialists from various fields of epigraphy.

Bearing in mind this, we have organized the agenda of this meeting in Bari, thanks to the precious support of dr. Anita Rocco, evaluating those fields of epigraphy commonly considered, in some way, 'off the beaten tracks'.

We have therefore invited colleagues that are involved in projects of digitization and encoding of epigraphic documents – precisely 'at the borders' of the area of interest of the EAGLE Project (as written in our subtitle).

First of all, we have to consider these 'borders' from a chronological perspective. I draw your attention to two papers about two projects: one by Giulia Sarullo about the Archaic Latin Inscriptions between 7th and 5th cent. BC (*The Encoding Challenge of the ILA Project*) and the other by Luna Cacchioli and Alessandra Tiburzi, with the supervision of Nadia Cannata, about the Italian Middle Age vernacular inscriptions till the 14th cent AD, at the beginning of the Modern Age (*EDV - Italian Medieval Epigraphy in the Vernacular (9th - 15th c.): a new database*). These two projects, as far landmarks outside the external borders of ancient Greek and Latin epigraphy, define a very long time-span (more than 2000 years: 700 BC - 1500 AD) during which the realization, the use and the notion of 'written monuments' (according to a fitting definition of the inscriptions, see Manacorda 2000) are not always the same. On the contrary, they deeply changed: I do believe that the ways we used to encode inscriptions must consider their transformations from the standard model.

Maybe, many of us have a platonic idea when they say or hear the word 'inscription' or also 'epigraph': a white marble slab or block, with a brilliant blue sky as background, bearing letters wisely carved, corresponding to words in a perfect Latin or classical Greek. This image is not always true, not only in archaic times or in Late Antiquity, Middle Ages, or in Byzantium or in the Pre-islamic or Islamic world, but also in Greek and Roman "classical" world. I think that this is proved with particular evidence by Rebecca Benefiel and Holly Sypniewski's paper about the graffiti of *Herculaneum* (*Working with texts and images: The Graffiti of Herculaneum*).[3]

In my opinion, the graffiti (in every age: archaic, classical, medieval and after) will help us to light up the idea of our meeting: they lead us to ask ourselves several methodology questions, useful also for other kinds of inscriptions.

First of all, the difficulty in defining the physical dimensions of the material on which the graffiti are: what are their correct measures? They are indefinite, because the graffiti are scratched or engraved on various objects and surfaces, and in many places: sometimes they are not written on a wall (measurable, at last), but directly on rock surfaces: there are so many impressive examples, as for example in the Sacred Cave of St. Michael in Apulia, in Southern Italy (Figure 4).

In some cases, we can only record the dimensions of single letters; in this regard, the experience of the *Digital Archive for the Study of Pre-Islamic Arabian Inscriptions* (illustrated in the paper by Alessandra Avanzini, Annamaria De Santis, Daniele Marotta, Irene Rossi, *Is still Arabia at the margins of Digital Epigraphy? Challenges in the Digitization of the Pre-islamic Inscriptions in the project DASI*),[4] among which the so-called 'rock-inscriptions' are recurrent, can be very useful (as for other issues, of course, also about writing and language).

---

[3] See http://ancientgraffiti.wlu.edu/hgp/. I have also to remember, about this same topic ('anomalous' classical epigraphy), the important project led by José Remesal (University of Barcelona) on the Amphorae epigraphy (see DATABASE - CEIPAC Corpus informático del instrumentum domesticum, http://ceipac.gh.ub.es/), with all the issues about the formalization of this special epigraphic documentation. We previewed a lecture by J. M. Remesal at the meeting in Bari, but unfortunately he could not be present.
[4] See http://dasi.humnet.unipi.it/.

FIGURE 4. MONTE SANT'ANGELO (GARGANO, NORTHERN APULIA, ITALY). GRAFFITI ON THE ROCK IN THE SACRED CAVE OF ST.MICHAEL. 7TH - 8 CENT. AD (IMAGE DIPARTIMENTO DI STUDI UMANISTICI, UNIVERSITY OF BARI 'ALDO MORO').

The graffiti, such as they are, are *suo loco appliciti*: then, it is essential to describe and to encode their positioning, both in relation to the other ones on the same carrier, and to their general archaeological context, with the aim to define, respectively, their relative and absolute chronology. The *Ancient Graffiti Project* as well the *Epigraphic Database Bari* (which also records many epigraphs - graffiti or not - still in their original position), bring to our attention some questions and some answers - maybe useful to all of us - about the possible ways of recording the archaeological contexts of inscriptions: which features we have to consider, to describe, to encode? With which level of detail?

Other important issues which concern all kinds of inscriptions, are language and writing. Extemporaneous writers use in their scratched inscriptions a 'popular' speech and/or an ordinary writing (Figure 5), that often are very far from the accuracy we see in the standard inscriptions by professional stonecutters.

This phenomenon is recurrent - as well-known - in Christian and medieval inscriptions: we can read something about this issue (and about other ones) in the paper offered by Anita Rocco (*From officina lapidaria to D.I.Y.: encoding inscriptions from the Roman Catacombs*), as like in the one by the équipe of Nadia Cannata.

I do not know which is the best way to encode the 'unusual' (not incorrect!) words and writings we meet in the inscriptions. But I am sure that this 'technical' issue (in this case as well as in other ones) implies an ontological reflexion by both epigraphers and IT experts.

Figure 5. Rome, via Ardeatina, catacomb of Domitilla. Graffito in cursive writing. ICVR, III 8034; EDB24880. First half of 4th cent. AD (image Epigraphic Database Bari and Papal Commission of Sacred Archaeology)

Which is the proper aim of the transcriptions of the inscribed texts by the epigraphers?

As for the language issue, my opinion is that, firstly, we should transcribe the texts as they are; then, in some way, we should adapt them to a 'correct' language - both ancient and modern - 'correct' only because it represents a common background of users of the different digital corpus of inscriptions.

As for the writing issue, I think that the opportunity to use many digital images can be a huge help: nevertheless we have to catalogue the images and the various features of writing, in order to retrieve the documents, according to the very often neglected point of view of palaeography. A few months ago, I talked about this issue during a workshop organized by the committee of the corpus of the *Inscriptiones Medi Aevi Italiae* at the Centro Italiano di Studi sull'Alto Medioevo in Spoleto: unfortunately, a shared inventory of the terms defining different kinds of ancient and medieval writings does not exist yet: maybe, the experience in EAGLE about shared controlled vocabularies in relation to carriers, materials, and so on, could be useful to this purpose.

FIGURE 6. ROME, VIA ARDEATINA, CATACOMB OF DOMITILLA. ICVR, III 7306; EDB24027. END OF 3RD CENT. AD (IMAGE EPIGRAPHIC DATABASE BARI AND PAPAL COMMISSION OF SACRED ARCHAEOLOGY)

FIGURE 7. TRANI (APULIA, ITALY), CATHEDRAL. IMAGES AND TEXTS SCRATCHED ON A FUNERARY LIMESTONE SLAB (FROM CARLETTI 1988). 7TH - 8TH CENT. AD (IMAGE DIPARTIMENTO DI STUDI UMANISTICI, UNIVERSITY OF BARI 'ALDO MORO').

Let's go back once more to the graffiti for a last issue (all of you can see how many are the issues for the epigraphers...): often we come across graffiti without any text or single letters (Figures 6-7).

May we consider them still as 'inscriptions', or not? We should ask ourselves the same question also in relation to many other 'unusual' documents traced on carriers in durable materials (according to another, old-fashioned, definition of the inscriptions) in different times and cultures.

In this respect, I would like to point out that the common idea of a structured relationship between texts and images in the inscriptions of the Classical world, maybe is not always true, as displayed in in the paper of Hannah Cornwell and Jane Masséglia, in relation to the documents considered in the Ashmolean Latin Inscriptions Project (*Signs, Symbols and Spaces in the Ashmolean Latin Collection*).[5]

The difficulty in describing and encoding the multifaceted relationship between texts and images is particularly high, both in Christian and Western Middle Ages inscriptions, but also - impressively - in the Byzantine world (see now a very interesting book: Eastmond 2015). The paper offered by Andreas Rhoby about the present status of projects of digitizing Byzantine inscriptions *(Challenges of Byzantine Epigraphy in the 21st Century)* obviously can not deal with all the issues about the very complex field of the Byzantine epigraphy (see Rhoby 2015): but, I think that the wide and strong experience of the EAGLE project can be very useful for the future digital corpus of these very important (and in many cases very *unusual*) inscriptions.

Facing these - and many other - questions raised by the 'off the beaten track' epigraphy implies a thorough analysis, to be carried out both by epigraphers and IT scholars, together.

As we have learned from our experience in the EAGLE project, this cooperation implies not only mere technical solutions, but can open the doors to new questions and new approaches to our documents, that can be seen under unexpected points of view, that the scholars of the IT domain can usefully offer to the epigraphers and generally to the scholars of the past (an example can be offered by Pio - Fumarola - Felle - Malerba - Ceci 2014).

I do believe that IT scholars could open the perspectives of the epigraphers to current orientations of our common field of research in the next future.

---

[5] http://www.ashmolean.org/ashwpress/latininscriptions/category/latin-inscriptions/.

Bibliography

Carletti, C. 1988. Graffiti di Trani. *Vetera Christianorum* 25: 585-604.

Eastmond, A. (ed.) 2015. *Viewing Inscriptions in the Late Antique and Medieval World*, New York, Cambridge University Press.

Manacorda, D. 2000. *Archeologia ed epigrafia: problemi di metodo a proposito di CIL*, VI, 8960, in A. Buko, A., Urbańczyk, P. (eds.), 2000. *Archeologia w teorii i w praktyce*: 277-293. Warszawa, Polskiej Akad. Nauk, Instytut Archeologii i Etnologii.

Pio, G., Fumarola, F., Felle, A. E., Malerba D. and Ceci, M. 2014. Discovering Novelty Patterns from the Ancient Christian Inscriptions of Rome. *Journal on Computing and Cultural Heritage* 7: 22, 1-21. doi: 10.1145/2629513 http://dl.acm.org/citation.cfm?doid=2669619.2629513

Rhoby, A. (ed.) 2015. *Inscriptions in Byzantium and Beyond. Methods - Projects - Case Studies*. Wien, Verlag der Österreichischen Akademie der Wissenschaften.

Schwabe, M. and Lifshitz, B. 1974. *Beth She'arim, II: The Greek Inscriptions*. New Brunswick NJ (USA), Rutgers University.

The Encoding Challenge of the ILA Project

Giulia Sarullo
Iscrizioni Latine Arcaiche - University of Enna 'Kore'

The ILA Project (Iscrizioni Latine Arcaiche)[1] consists in the digital edition of the Latin inscriptions found in the *Latium vetus* – with the exception of the *Vendia*'s Urn found in Cerveteri and the Garigliano bowl – dating back to the period between the 7th and the 5th century BC. The corpus, consisting of only a few documents of a certain length at the beginning of the 20th century, has grown significantly since 1950s reaching the total of shortly less than a hundred texts.[2]

The majority of the inscriptions in the collection are *frustuli* – some consisting of only one letter – whose relevance resides in their preserving an evidence of various uses of writing in Latium at the early stages of its history. On the other hand, among the longer texts this corpus counts some of the most complex inscriptions in Latin epigraphy, such as the Forum Romanum inscription (CIL, I^2 1), the *Duenos* vase (CIL, I^2 4), the Tibur pedestal inscription (CIL, I^2 2658), and the *Lapis Satricanus* (CIL, I^2 2832a), to name but a few renowned examples. The complexity of these texts chiefly depends on three factors, descending from their antiquity: the state of preservation of the text-bearing object, the presence of peculiar epigraphic uses (i.e. fluctuating direction of writing, orientation of the letters, etc.) not attested in later inscriptions, and the linguistic phase documented by the texts. These factors are closely related to the steps that lead to the edition of a text: first we try to read what remains of the text (and what is readable chiefly depends on the physical conditions of the support) identifying the direction of writing and other possible unusual epigraphic practices, then we try to interpret the meaning of the text. It goes without saying that an inscription corrupted by lacunae or lacking portions of text will be more difficult to understand, more so in the cases of epigraphic documents recording a linguistic phase so scantly attested and, as a consequence, so arduous to reconstruct.

How do these issues influence the implementation of a digital edition of the archaic Latin inscriptions?

As explained in Sarullo (2011: 157-159) and in Rocca, Sarullo and Muscariello (in print: §4), we decided to digitize the archaic Latin inscriptions following the

---

[1] On the ILA Project, still in progress, see Muscariello 2011; Sarullo 2011 and, more recently, Rocca, Sarullo and Muscariello in print.
[2] At the moment, it is not possible to determine a precise number in that the discovery of new inscriptions has been announced but these have not been published yet.

EpiDoc Guidelines,³ a set of recommendations for XML markup of epigraphic documents according to Leiden's convention (Krummrey and Panciera 1980) that is now the point of reference for digital epigraphic projects. EpiDoc is also the standard chosen for the aggregation of the data of EDR, EDB, EDH and HE in the recently constituted *Europeana Network of Ancient Greek and Latin Epigraphy* (EAGLE),⁴ in which the archaic Latin inscriptions corpus will also converge.

According to the EpiDoc Guidelines, the encoding process of epigraphic documents aims for the creation of a digital edition of an inscription (or a corpus of inscriptions) by providing all information about the text and the text-bearing object in a semantic markup. Specific tags are used to illustrate the physical conditions of the support – as well as its provenance and dating – and the inscription, for which a description is provided (position of the inscription, measurement of the letters, execution techniques, punctuation), together with the transcription of the text, that records all the features that can characterize an epigraphic document (lacunae, abbreviations, overstruck letters, etc.).

In consideration of the above mentioned factors, the encoding of the archaic Latin inscriptions poses a challenge to the digital epigraphist because of the peculiar characteristics that distinguish them from later epigraphic documents and, for this reason, have not been taken into consideration in the EpiDoc Guidelines yet. Nevertheless, the extensible nature of the XML allow us to create new values, if necessary, in order to account for situations unaccounted for up to now.

We will here focus our attention on two specific issues that are exemplary in this respect: the direction of writing and the orientation of the letters.

Direction of writing

The EpiDoc Guidelines (http://www.stoa.org/epidoc/gl/latest/trans-linebreakdirection.html) provide two possible values for the @rend attribute of the <lb/> element to indicate the direction of writing of each line of inscription: "left-to-right" and "right-to-left". This markup does not affect the display of the letters in the transcription of the text – that will always be written from left to right – but the actual direction of writing will be indicated by an arrow next to each line. The authors of the Guidelines specify that "left-to-right" is the default value, in that it is the most frequent direction of the text in the epigraphic documents dated after the 4th century BC. In the ILA Project no value can be set as default, in that the Latin inscriptions dating back to the 7th and 6th century BC show a fluctuating trend: there are left-to-right inscriptions, such as the *Vendia*'s Urn inscription;

---

³ For further information on EpiDoc and its history, see Elliott 2007 and Elliott, Bodard, Cayless et al. 2006-2013. The guidelines are available at http://www.stoa.org/epidoc/gl/latest/.
⁴ On the relationship between EAGLE projects and EpiDoc see Felle 2012.

right-to-left epigraphs, such as the Duenos inscription; boustrophedon, such as the Forum inscription, in which every line will be marked with an appropriate value; and there are also some exceptional cases such as the Castor and Pollux dedication from Lavinium (CIL, I² 2833) and the Tibur pedestal inscription (CIL, I² 2658).

The last three examples require the creation of specific values (not provided in the EpiDoc Guidelines yet) in order to account for the unusual directions of writing they present. We will begin our discussion with the Forum inscription, that is perhaps one of the most famous documents in our corpus. This text is cut vertically on a stone pillar in boustrophedon, but the alternation in the direction of writing shows some irregularities.

As described in Sarullo (2015: 69-70),

> The inscription begins from the bottom right angle and goes on clockwise in regular boustrophedon for 7 lines (3 on side A, 4 on side B); in starting the first line of side C (line 8), the mason probably changed his position and continued writing from right to left: thus the lettering results upside-down in comparison with those of line 7 […]. Line 9 is upside-down as well, but from left to right; only in line 10 is the correct orientation of writing restored with a capsizing of the lettering.

The same happens in the passage from line 15 to line 16, where letters are upside-down once again. This procedure was described as 'false boustrophedon' by Jeffery (1990: 49), in that there is no actual change in the direction of writing in passing from one line to the next (Figure 1).

For this reason, the markup of lines 8, 9 and 16 cannot be carried out by simply using the provided values ("left-to-right" and "right-to-left"), in that they would not be sufficient to account for the peculiar orientation of these lines. New values for the @rend attribute are then necessary, and we decided to create two variations of the existing values, i.e. "ud-left-to-right" and "ud-right-to-left", where 'ud' stands for 'upside-down'. In the XSLT, each value of the @rend attribute referring to the direction of a line is associated with an arrow actually indicating the direction of writing in the resulting HTML (e.g. → or ←). It is then necessary to find specific Unicode characters that could adequately represent the new values; a possible solution can be found in the two signs in Figure 2.

The Forum inscription presents another irregularity as regards the boustrophedon: the last line of side C (line 11) and the first of side D (line 12) are both retrograde, thus interrupting the alternation in the direction of writing. Nevertheless, this

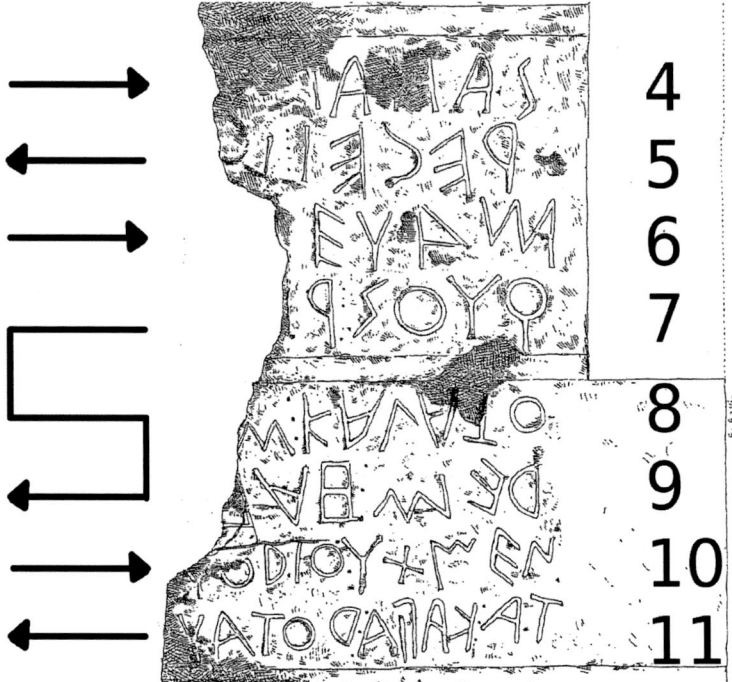

FIGURE 1. THE FORUM INSCRIPTION, SIDE B AND C (APOGRAPH BY COMPARETTI 1900 ELABORATED BY THE AUTHOR)

Symbol	Unicode	HTML Escape Code	@rend value
↪	U+21AA	&#8618;	"ud-left-to-right"
↩	U+21A9	&#8617;	"ud-right-to-left"

FIGURE 2. UNICODE CHARACTERS REPRESENTING THE UPSIDE-DOWN DIRECTIONS OF WRITING.

anomaly does not create any difficulties in the markup in that both lines are marked as "right-to-left".

The second example showing an unusual course of the lettering is the bronze lamina from Lavinium with a dedication to Castor and Pollux (Figure 3). The inscription runs right-to-left, but at the end of the first line, perhaps for lack of space (Bloch 1960: 187), the author rotated the lamina 90 degrees clockwise and engraved the two vowels of the conjunction *-que* down the left side, in a right-to-left direction, with the tops of the letters toward the edge of the plate. In the encoding process we treated these two vowels as a separate line in order to point out the different direction of writing, thus raising the number of lines to three.

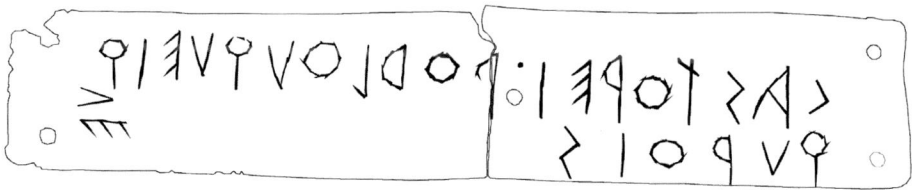

FIGURE 3. THE LAMINA FROM LAVINIUM (APOGRAPH BY G. SARULLO).

FIGURE 4. THE TIBUR PEDESTAL INSCRIPTION (APOGRAPH BY MANCINI 1979)

A more complex case is that of the Tibur pedestal inscription (Figure 4), whose letters follow a serpentine course. This text is marked up as seven different lines and each line is specified by the attribute of the direction of writing.

The EpiDoc Guidelines do not offer a specific value to identify the 'spilled' letters (Jeffery 1990: 46), such as those attested in the lamina from Lavinium, or the serpentine course of the Tibur pedestal inscription. At first, we defined these particular courses of the lettering with the elements <lb rend="up-to-down"/> and <lb rend="up-to-down"/> (see Sarullo 2011: 165-167).

As a matter of fact, these choices result inaccurate, in that "up-to-down" would rather describe a line in which letters run from the top to the bottom of the epigraphic field but retaining the horizontal orientation and, in the same way, "down-to-up" would describe a line in which the letters run from the bottom to the top retaining the horizontal orientation; furthermore, a definition such as

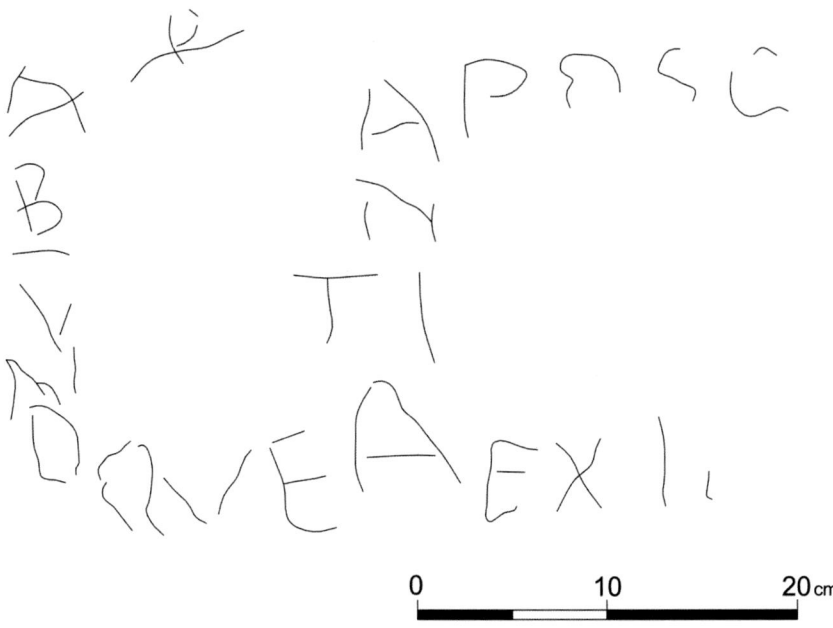

FIGURE 5. INSCRIPTION FROM THE CEMETERY OF COMMODILLA IN ROME, ICVR, II, 6117 - EDB19242 (FROM ROCCO 2005: 296).

"up-to-down" or "down-to-up" would not have provided any information about the actual direction of the lettering. These considerations are the result of a comparison between the archaic Latin inscriptions and the epigraphs of EDB as regards the direction of writing – and I would like to dearly thank Anita Rocco for the stimulating discussion on the subject – in that some of their inscriptions show exactly these kinds of course (together with many other very unusual directions), see for example Figure 5.

New values are then necessary to describe situations such as those here mentioned in the most accurate way possible. We would like to suggest "cwr-left-to-right" and "ccwr-left-to-right" and their counterparts "cwr-right-to-left" and "ccwr-right-to-left", where 'cwr' stands for 'clockwise rotated' and 'ccwr' for 'counterclockwise rotated' to indicate in which direction the course of the inscription rotates. Although, as of today, only "cwr-right-to-left" and "ccwr-right-to-left" will be used in the ILA Project, it seems preferable, from the methodological point of view, to provide a complete range of values that can account for all the possibilities. To these new values of the @rend attribute we can associate the Unicode characters showed in Figure 6.

Symbol	Unicode	HTML Escape Code	@rend value
⬌	U+2B0E	&#11022;	"cwr-left-to-right"
⬑	U+2B11	&#11025;	"ccwr-left-to-right"
⬏	U+2B0F	&#11023;	"cwr-right-to-left"
⬐	U+2B10	&#11024;	"ccwr-right-to-left"

FIGURE 6. UNICODE CHARACTERS REPRESENTING ROTATED DIRECTIONS OF WRITING.

Symbol	Unicode	HTML Escape Code
↴	U+21B4	&#8628;
⤵	U+2935	&#10549;

FIGURE 7. OTHER SUITABLE UNICODE CHARACTERS NOT AVAILABLE IN ALL THE DIRECTIONS NEEDED.

Unfortunately, at the moment the shapes that would seem more appropriate for our purposes (Figure 7), do not exist for all the directions we need.

A final note about the direction of writing of the Tibur pedestal inscription. Because of an unfortunate coincidence, the vertically cut lines 3 and 5 are both damaged, so that only vestiges of letters remain in line 3, whereas in line 5 the lacuna covers the space of a letter, for which scholars supply an O in order to read the word D/[O]NO/M. For these corrupted lines the direction of writing has been reconstructed as right-to-left for analogy with the other two vertically cut lines of the inscription, i.e. line 1 and line 7. Nevertheless, line 5 presents an awkward situation. Of the three letters originally composing the line, only two remains, N and O: the first one is cut horizontally, and not vertically as one would expect it to be, while the second one cannot give any hint as to the direction of the line because of its round shape. A doubt can then arise as to how to interpret this line: shall we consider it a clockwise rotated right-to-left line as line 1 (with a rotated N, then, on line 5) or shall we consider it a down-to-up line? This text offers many examples of letters that are cut in a direction different than that of the line they are in, so that a rotated N would not result so out-of-place here. Nevertheless, it is probably more realistic to think that the author cut the letters from the bottom to the top in a vertical line. For this reason, we decided to define the direction of writing of this line as "down-to-up".

The partial encoding of the lamina from Lavinium and the Tibur pedestal inscription can be seen in Figure 8 and Figure 9.

```
CASTOREI PODLOVQVEIQ/VE/QVROIS

<lb n="1" rend="right-to-left"/>CASTOREIPODLOVQEIQ
<lb n="2" rend="ccwr-right-to-left"/>VE
<lb n="3" rend="right-to-left"/>QVROIS
```

FIGURE 8. PARTIAL MARKUP OF THE INSCRIPTION ON THE LAMINA FROM LAVINIUM.

```
HOIM/EDMITATKAVIO/[S---]/ONIOSQETIOSD/[O]NO/MPROFILEO/D

<lb n="1" rend="cwr-right-to-left"/>HOIM
<lb n="2" rend="right-to-left"/>ED<hi rend="reversed">M</hi>ITATKA<hi
    rend="upside-down">V</hi>IO
<lb n="3" rend="ccwr-right-to-left"/><supplied reason="lost">S</supplied>
    <gap reason="lost" extent="unknown" unit="character"/>
<lb n="4" rend="left-to-right"/>O<hi rend="reversed">N</hi>IOSQETIOSD
<lb n="5" rend="down-to-up"/><supplied reason="lost">O</supplied>
    <unclear reason="damage">N</unclear>O
<lb n="6" rend="right-to-left"/>MPROFI<hi rend="upside-down">L</hi>EO
<lb n="7" rend="ccwr-right-to-left"/>D
```

FIGURE 9. PARTIAL MARKUP OF THE TIBUR PEDESTAL INSCRIPTION.

Orientation of the letters

With the term 'orientation' we refer to the relationship between the course of a line of writing and the directions in which a letter is inscribed. In these respects, the ILA corpus provides us with examples of reversed letters (written in direction opposite to the one of the line) and upside-down letters.

Reversed letters are not a unique feature of the archaic Latin inscriptions, in that there are some examples of this phenomenon, called *litterae inversae*, also in later epigraphic documents, where the initial letter of an abbreviated word is written as reversed in order to avoid misunderstandings of gender. One of the most famous examples is the reversed *C* for *mulier* 'woman' (literally *Caia*), used in the onomastic formula of freedmen or freedwomen (between the *nomen gentilicium* and the *cognomen*) to signal that the individual was the slave of the woman whose *gentilicium* he or she bore (see Figure 10); another instance is the reversed *F* for *femina / filia* (Di Stefano Manzella 1987: 151-152).

The EpiDoc Guidelines provide us with an element to mark up these particular cases, that is <hi rend="reversed">. As a matter of fact, when the standard EpiDoc XSLT is applied, a letter marked up with this element would be enclosed

FIGURE 10. DETAIL OF CIL, I2 1799 (EDR147038), ELABORATED BY THE AUTHOR
(FROM CIL: TAV. 84, NO. 3).

in double round parenthesis in the resulting HTML, as suggested by Panciera[5] for the cases in which the editor writes something different from what is actually on the stone not as a correction but as a sort of transposition, as in the case of the *litterae inversae*.

Following to the convention established by Panciera, then, a reversed *C* will be transcribed with the word *mulier* (inflected according to the required morpho-syntactical function) enclosed in double parenthesis, as can be seen in the edition of the inscription shown in Figure 10 (CIL, I² 1799, EDR147038):

Novia ((mulieris)) l(iberta)
Delpis; fei=
lei posierunt

---

[5] 'Appare inoltre opportuno introdurre un nuovo segno (( )), per contraddistinguere unitariamente tutta una serie di casi in cui l'editore scrive qualcosa di diverso da ciò che sta sulla pietra e questo non per correzione o aggiunta, ma per ricorso ad una sorta di equivalenza o trasposizione, come nel caso delle litterae claudiane, la cui resa era rimasta sin qui sostanzialmente irrisolta, oppure nel caso delle litterae inversae, delle notae verborum vel numerorum, degli anaglypha', Panciera 2006b: 1722; see also Panciera 2006a.

FIGURE 11. THE TIBUR PEDESTAL INSCRIPTION (PHOTOGRAPH BY MARTA MUSCARIELLO, ELABORATED BY THE AUTHOR IN ORDER TO HIGHLIGHT REVERSED AND UPSIDE-DOWN LETTERS).

In archaic Latin epigraphy reversed letters are quite common, especially N and S, but, contrary to what happens in later testimonies, they do not carry any particular meaning. It is possible to consider them as a consequence of the inconstancy of the direction of writing that characterizes the archaic Latin inscriptions, as it has been shown above. In printed editions these letters are left unmarked and we decided to comply to this practice; nevertheless, we chose to use the <hi rend="reversed"> element anyway in encoding these texts so that in a search it would be possible to recover all the inscriptions presenting a reversed letter.

The alternation in the direction of writing could be responsible for another alteration in the orientation of the letters, that is the upside-down letters. The origin of this phenomenon has been recently explained as the result of an influence of a Paleo-Umbrian/Sabine model (Maras 2009a: 432; 2009b: 111). As a matter of fact, this phenomenon is attested in the above mentioned Tibur pedestal inscription (see Figure 11), where the letter O is reduced to a dot, a hole in the stone, a typical feature of the South-Picene epigraphic traditions.

Since the upside-down letters appear only in a small amount of texts dating to the 7th and 6th century BC and are not attested in later epigraphy, the EpiDoc

Guidelines do not provide for these eventualities and none of the allowed values of @rend for the <hi> element are suitable for an accurate rendering of these issues. We need to provide therefore a new one, i.e. "upside-down", in order to render, for example, the V (line 2) and the L (line 6) in the Tibur pedestal inscription.

As in the case of reversed letters, the markup of this peculiarity will not influence the appearance of the letters in the edition of the text, but it will result useful to recover all instances of letters written in an orientation different from the expected one.

Conclusion

The challenge that these ancient texts poses to the digital epigraphist is proportional to the one a traditional epigraphist has to face when working on them. The considerations expressed so far are the outcome of the encoding process of the archaic Latin inscriptions, a process that is still in progress and still requires an effort on the part of the encoder in order to deal with all the issues connected with these epigraphs. Nevertheless, a lot has been done and we wanted to share here some partial results of this work, in order to submit to the attention of the scientific community the solutions that we have devised. Although these new values were specifically designed to account for the peculiarities of our corpus, it is not impossible that they could be of some use in the encoding of other 'off the beaten track' epigraphic corpora.

Bibliography

Bloch, R. 1960. L'origine du culte des Dioscures à Rome. *RPh* 34 (troisième série): 182-193.

Comparetti, D. 1900. Iscrizione arcaica del Foro Romano. Firenze-Roma, Tipografia dei Fratelli Bencini.

Di Stefano Manzella, I. 1987. Mestiere di Epigrafista. Guida alla schedatura del materiale epigrafico lapideo. Roma, Edizioni Quasar.

Elliott, T., Bodard, G. and Cayless, H. *et al.* 2006-2016. EpiDoc: Epigraphic Documents in TEI XML. Online material. http://epidoc.sf.net.

Elliot, T. 2007. Conformance and Interoperability: What it means to be EpiDoc. http://www.stoa.org/epidoc/gl/5/conformance.html.

Felle, A. E. 2012. Esperienze diverse e complementari nel trattamento digitale delle fonti epigrafiche: il caso di EAGLE ed EpiDoc. In N. Palazzolo (ed.), *Diritto romano e scienze antichistiche nell'era digitale*. Convegno di studio (Firenze, 12-13 settembre 2011), Collectanea Graeco-Romana. Studi e strumenti per la ricerca storico-giuridica, 10: 117-130. Torino, Giappichelli.

Jeffery, L. H. 1990. The Local Scripts of Archaic Greece. A Study of the Origin of the Greek Alphabet and its Development from the eighth to the fifth centuries B.C. Oxford, Oxford University Press.

Krummrey, H. and Panciera, S. 1980. Criteri di edizione e segni diacritici. *Tituli* 2: 205-215.

Mahoney, A. 2006. Epigraphy. In L. Burnad, K. O'Brian O'Keeffe and J. Unsworth (eds.), *Electronic Textual Editing*: 224-237. New York, Modern Language Association of America.

Mancini, A. 1979. L'iscrizione sulla base di Tivoli CIL, I^2 2658. Nuova lettura. *Rivista di epigrafia italica, Studi etruschi* XLVII: 370-375.

Maras, D. F. 2009a. Caratteri dell'epigrafia latina arcaica del Lazio meridionale. In L. Drago Troccoli (ed.), *Il Lazio dai Colli Albani ai Monti Lepini tra preistoria ed età moderna*: 431-439. Roma, Quasar.

Maras, D. F. 2009b. Novità sulla diffusione dell'alfabeto latino nel Lazio arcaico. In F. Mannino, M. Mannino, and D. F. Maras (eds.), *Theodor Mommsen e il Lazio antico. Giornata di Studi in memoria dell'illustre storico, epigrafista e giurista* (Terracina, Sala Valadier, 3 aprile 2004): 105-118. Roma, "L'Erma" di Bretschneider.

Muscariello, M. 2011. L'edizione digitale dei testi epigrafici come strumento di ricerca. II Qualche nota sul progetto Iscrizioni Latine Arcaiche. In P. Cotticelli Kurras (ed.), *Linguistica e Filologia digitale. Aspetti e progetti*: 133-147. Alessandria, Edizioni dell'Orso.

Panciera, S. 2006a. Segni diacritici: riflessioni e proposte. In S. Panciera, *Epigrafi, Epigrafia, Epigrafisti. Scritti vari editi e inediti (1956-2005) con note complementari e indici*, II: 1711-1717. Roma, Edizioni Quasar.

Panciera, S. 2006b. I segni diacritici: dieci anni dopo. In S. Panciera, *Epigrafi, Epigrafia, Epigrafisti. Scritti vari editi e inediti (1956-2005) con note complementari e indici*, II: 1717-1726. Roma, Edizioni Quasar.

Rocca, G., Sarullo, G. and Muscariello, M. In print. The Digital Edition of the Archaic Latin Inscriptions (7th -5th century B.C.). In *EAGLE2016. International Conference on Digital and Traditional Epigraphy in Context* (Rome, 27-29 January 2016).

Rocco, A. 2005. Le iscrizioni 'a nastro' nel cimitero di Commodilla a Roma. *Atti della Pontificia Accademia Romana di Archeologia. Memorie*, III serie in 8°, VI: 263-445.

Sarullo, G. 2011. L'edizione digitale dei testi epigrafici come strumento di ricerca. III The Encoding of the Archaic Latin Inscriptions. In P. Cotticelli Kurras (ed.), *Linguistica e Filologia digitale. Aspetti e progetti*: 157-169. Alessandria, Edizioni dell'Orso.

Sarullo, G. 2015. Boustrophedic writing on *cippi*. In E. Dupraz and W. Sowa (eds.), *Genres épigraphiques et langues d'attestation fragmentaire dans l'espace méditerranéen*, Cahiers de l'ERIAC 9 – Fonctionnements linguistiques: 69-81, Mont-Saint-Agnan Presses Universitaires de Rouen et du Havre.

Images and Text on the Walls of Herculaneum: Designing the Ancient Graffiti Project

Rebecca R. Benefiel* and Holly M. Sypniewski**
Ancient Graffiti Project
*Washington & Lee University and **Millsaps College

The Ancient Graffiti Project team is currently studying, re-editing, and creating digital records in the Epigraphic Database Roma for a particular group of inscriptions: the thousands of informal, handwritten wall-inscriptions, also known as ancient graffiti, which were scratched into the wall-plaster of Roman towns. Nearly five hundred of these handwritten inscriptions have been documented at Herculaneum, while several thousand have been collected in Pompeii. In addition to contributing these inscriptions to the Epigraphic Database Roma (http://www.edr-edr.it), we are also creating a linked resource, the Ancient Graffiti Project search engine (http://agp.wlu.edu), which will allow users to conduct location-specific searches for graffiti, and will provide additional search options that complement the capabilities of EDR and EAGLE Europeana (http://www.eagle-network.eu/).

Among the many texts written on the walls of these two cities, there sometimes also appear graffiti drawings, or figural graffiti. These hand-drawn, incised sketches can occur in conjunction with text, or they may appear independently, as stand-alone drawings. Gladiators, for example, were one topic of great interest. A graffito from the House of the Ceii in Pompeii depicts both text and image, with two figures of gladiators identified by labels giving their names and the number of their victories (Figure 1).

Other drawings might stand alone. At Pompeii, a drawing of a gladiator was discovered in the House of the Faun, alongside two others (Figure 2; no sketches were made for the other figures). None of the three were labeled or featured associated text. At Herculaneum, the House of the Stags is so named for the fact that a number of figural graffiti found there depict deer. Sometimes these are individual drawings of deer; other times the drawings include additional details, such as a hunter or a dog pursuing the deer. These too are inscribed simply as drawings, again without text.[1]

These figural graffiti have provided us with several challenges as we digitize them for the Epigraphic Database Roma and as we design a way to search for

---

[1] For an excellent study of the House of the Stags (Casa dei Cervi), see Tan Timh 1988. We have processed these figural graffiti and contributed them to EDR, where they are now available: EDR145004 - EDR145008, EDR145764, EDR145765, and EDR145766.

FIGURE 1. GRAFFITO OF GLADIATORS FROM POMPEII (CIL, IV 8055A AND 8055B)

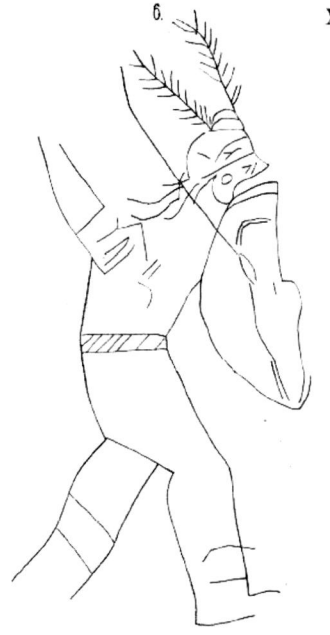

FIGURE 2. DRAWING OF A GLADIATOR, MENTIONED AT CIL, IV 1481A (FROM GARRUCCI 1856, TAB. XV 6)

and retrieve such drawings via the Ancient Graffiti Project search engine. In this article, we discuss the challenges we face and some of the strategies we have developed in response, with a particular focus on the material from Herculaneum.[2]

---

[2] The ancient graffiti from Herculaneum are published at CIL, IV 2513-2513a, 2521, 2543, 5449, 10478-10717; Della Corte 1958; Guadagno 1983 and 1988; Varone 2000 and 2012. For Herculaneum more generally, see also Wallace-Hadrill 2011, and Guidobaldi and Esposito 2012.

Our Material

It was much more common in Herculaneum and Pompeii for someone to write a message on a wall than to sketch a drawing. People wrote their names, greetings to friends, quotations of literature, and many other types of messages, resulting in the thousands of inscriptions that have been discovered on the walls of these towns. However, a smaller but not insignificant number of drawings were also inscribed. Rarely does one find a large scene, like the illustration of a gladiatorial contest with athletes, musicians, and perhaps magistrates, sketched by hand on a funerary monument just outside the Porta Nocera of Pompeii (Figure 3).[3] More often, people made small sketches on the walls around them, choosing from among a handful of popular designs: heads in profile, boats, gladiators, animals, and geometric designs.[4] Herculaneum features figural graffiti of all these types.

FIGURE 3. A SCENE DEPICTING A GLADIATORIAL EVENT, SKETCHED ON A TOMB OUTSIDE THE PORTA NOCERA AT POMPEII (CIL, IV 10237)

In Herculaneum, we are fortunate that a significant number of graffiti are still extant and *in situ*, since roofing has been reconstructed for many buildings in the excavations, to protect them from the elements. In those instances, we are able to study and work with the graffito itself, along with its publication in the *Corpus Inscriptionum Latinarum*, vol. IV. Yet due to the fragile nature of wall plaster, many graffiti that were recorded previously have now been lost. This is especially true in Pompeii, where large, open-air excavations began early on.

Much of our data for figural graffiti, therefore, from both Pompeii and Herculaneum, consists of verbal descriptions of graffiti that have now disappeared. Working

---
[3] D31 in Cooley and Cooley 2014; cf. also CIL, IV 10236 and 10238 drawn nearby.
[4] For a full catalogue of figural graffiti from across the Mediterranean world, see Langner 2001.

with this legacy data presents a range of issues. Furthermore, the different editors of CIL vol. IV and its supplemental issues over the past century and a half have used different methods to denote that a drawing was present, and their practices have changed over time. Figural graffiti, for example, might be:

a. mentioned or depicted directly within a CIL entry,
b. noted in the introduction to a CIL entry,
c. noted in the apparatus of a CIL entry, or
d. omitted by CIL.

Descriptions of figural graffiti within an entry of CIL

A drawing could, for example, be described in the text field of an entry in CIL vol. IV. This scenario occurs in the entries below, where three drawings of human heads (CIL, IV 2315-2316) and two drawings of gladiators (CIL, IV 2319) are described in small italics, while the Latin text of the inscription is presented in capital letters. The descriptions of the figural graffiti are placed where the images occur, in relation to the textual inscriptions (Figure 4).

This practice is common in the original volume of CIL vol. IV (published 1871), when it seems that the editors documented textual and figural graffiti that were in close proximity, or that were in some way related to each other. Printing practices at the time did not allow for copious illustration. Line-drawings depicting the appearance of the *text* of ancient graffiti were included in tables at the end of that

| 2315. 2316 in faucium pariete dexteriore, in tectorio rubro, litteris cursivis, M alta est 0,003 m.

        2315   2316
        SIMIVS
hominis   *hominis*   *hominis*
caput   *caput*   *caput*
                 SIICVNDVS
                 HΓWN

2316 dedi tab. XXXVII 9. Descripsi.
  2316 v. 2 non expedio (nisi forte litterae sunt H, L, M, N sine ratione compositae), nec v. 1 lectionis est omnino certae, cum alienis lineis confusus sit. | 2319 ad sinistram capitum illorum (v. 2315) inferius.

              IANOYA[PIOYC]
              INPE PAT*V*[RICS
              XI LX
gladi-   *gladi-*
ator   *ator*
scudo et
gladio breti
armatus

Tab. XXXVII 8 ex meo apographo.
  1 male scriptus ideoque lectionis ambiguae est, maxime in altera parte, quam uncis inclusi. — 2 V[parum clarae sunt.
                                                          10 |

FIGURE 4. THE ENTRIES OF CIL, IV 2315-2316 AND 2319, REPRESENTING FIGURAL GRAFFITI VIA BRIEF DESCRIPTION IN ITALICS

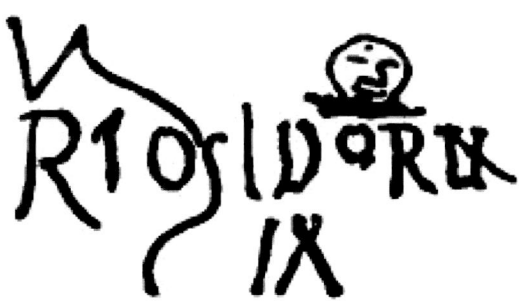

FIGURE 5. LINE-DRAWING DEPICTING BOTH TEXT AND IMAGE FROM HERCULANEUM (CIL, IV 10493)

original volume. However, these line-drawings rarely depict the figural graffiti.[5] Rather, interest laid squarely on the text of inscriptions.[6]

In later supplements, line-drawings for figural graffiti were sometimes included in the CIL entry when the drawings and text were obviously understood as one inscription (as shown in Figure 1, above). With the complications and costs associated with preparing and printing illustrations, however, it also remained common practice to represent figural graffiti with very brief description in italics (e.g. CIL, IV 4822, 4823, 5264, 5275, 6624, 6672, 6889). Only one example from Herculaneum in CIL includes a line-drawing of a figural graffito, a reproduction of a sketch prepared a century earlier of an inscription that had since disappeared (Figure 5).[7]

Figural graffiti described in notes or apparatus

The most common strategy for documenting figural graffiti in CIL vol. IV is by including brief mention of a drawing somewhere other than the main field. Such mention might occur either in the editorial note that introduces an inscription or in the apparatus that follows it. In CIL, IV 10711, for example, the main field of the CIL entry gives the text of an alphabetic series (Figure 6). The introductory note gives the location of the inscription and remarks that, on that same southern wall of the *ala*, there were nearby drawings of nine gladiatorial helmets and a small phallus (*iuxta novem galeas gladiatorias et parvum phallum*). This manner

---

[5] A few examples of text that is inscribed and arranged in some sort of shape provide an exception (e.g. the name Psyche written in the shape of a heart, CIL, IV 1362, illustrated at Tab. XXVII 15).
[6] One might likewise note that the numbers 2315 and 2316 were assigned to the two pieces of text; the three drawings among which those texts are situated remain unnumbered, yet are contextually associated with both writings.
[7] By the time of publication, the graffito itself had been lost and even the original location was uncertain. As CIL, IV points out, it had been inscribed along the Decumanus Inferior, on the facade of either Insula II or VII.

10711 In aedibus V · 35, in alae (B apud Maiuri I p. 378 fig. 308) pariete meridionali, iuxta novem galeas gladiatorias et parvum phallum graphio delineata

0,37 ABCDIIFGHILMNOPQ 0,03

Della Corte p. 267 n. 321. Signa quaedam cernuntur, quae iam intellegi nequeunt.

FIGURE 6. CIL ENTRY FOR AN ALPHABETIC SERIES, WHICH APPEARED NEAR FIGURAL GRAFFITI (CIL, IV 10711)

of mentioning drawings in the introductory note becomes more common in the fascicles of CIL vol. IV produced in the later twentieth century and so the figural graffiti from Herculaneum are usually represented this way (cf. CIL, IV 10568, 10586, 10673, 10704).

The presence of a drawing might also be mentioned in the critical apparatus below the text field. This occurs at the entry for CIL, IV 10532, where it is noted that the three names of the inscription were each inscribed in the shape of a boat (v. 2-4 *scripti sunt ad phaseli formam*). With this mode of description, where figural graffiti are noted in the introduction or apparatus of a CIL entry and the inscription is presented without illustration, there is usually no information about where the drawing was in relation to the textual graffito. Indeed, it is often difficult to understand or reconstruct whether or not the text and drawings appeared in close proximity or simply in the same room. In the House of the Stags in Herculaneum, the connection between inscriptions mentioned in a single entry is even more tenuous. One textual inscription appears in a room on the second floor (CIL, IV 10561); in the apparatus, the editor notes that numerous figural graffiti (*nonnullas figuras graphio delineatas*) appeared not on the same wall, but on different walls *in a different room* on the second floor (Figure 7).[8] These include not just one or two figural graffiti, but a remarkable number of column bases, a gladiator, animals, and a number of stags or deer. Since there was no way to create an entry for CIL without Latin text, this association of numerous figural graffiti as linked to the one textual inscription in the next room over was the best that could be done.

---

[8] One must pay careful attention to catch that the name Onesimus appears in ambiente 4, while the many figural graffiti appear on the east and north walls of ambiente 5.

10561 In superiore tabulato, in *"ambiente n. 4 (già 55)"*, in pariete meridionali

| 0,317 | O N I I S I M V S | 0,04—0,073 |

Della Corte p. 253 n. 100.

Adnotat Della Corte p. 254 n. 109 in *"ambiente n. 5"* eiusdem superioris tabulati inesse nonnullas figuras graphio delineatas: in pariete orientali tres bases atticas, quarum tertiae superstat columna, ac gladiatorem; in pariete septentrionali cervos aliaque animalia et basim atticam; bases autem et columnam vidi in pariete orientali parvae cellae, quae est supra apothecam, quae n. 4 designatur apud Maiuri I p. 303 fig. 240.

FIGURE 7. CIL ENTRY FOR THE NAME ONESIMUS, WITH NUMEROUS FIGURAL GRAFFITI DESCRIBED IN THE APPARATUS (CIL, IV 10561)

Figural graffiti omitted by CIL

One other possibility exists as well, namely, when figural graffiti were not even mentioned in CIL. In each of the previous scenarios, the editors of CIL include a description of a figural graffito when it was in close proximity to a textual inscription. In contrast, figural graffiti found in isolation might be excluded altogether. Fortunately there is now a useful resource devoted to figural graffiti: Martin Langner's *Antike Graffitizeichnungen*, a monograph and accompanying CD-ROM with a database of figural graffiti from across the Mediterranean. His catalog includes some 600 graffiti drawings from Pompeii and 48 from Herculaneum; ca. 200 of these graffiti drawings are not mentioned in CIL.[9] Whenever possible, Langner will provide a line-drawing of the graffito, either his own or one found in an earlier source; therefore, his database includes line drawings that are not included in CIL even when a drawing is described. However, certain motifs are omitted from Langner's catalog. While he does catalog the more interesting *Phalluskopfen* examples, he generally omits simple drawings of *phalli*.[10] He also excludes from his collection the decorative elements of *coronae* and *palmae*, which are sometimes mentioned in CIL. This means that an accurate total of all figural graffiti in Pompeii and Herculaneum can only be reached by working through the collections of both Langner and CIL. To create the most comprehensive resource possible for figural graffiti, we include *all* known drawings in the AGP search engine.[11]

---

[9] For one example, see Figure 10, below, a drawing of a camel in the Samnite House at Herculaneum.

[10] Cf. CIL, IV 10568, 10604a, 10704, 10711, all drawings of phalli that do not appear in Langner's catalogue.

[11] As of January 1, 2016, we have made 40 figural graffiti from Herculaneum searchable and retrievable at agp.wlu.edu.

Documenting extant figural graffiti

Since the verbal descriptions of figural graffiti provided by legacy data are limited and vague or exceedingly general (e.g. *caput*), the best circumstance under which to digitize a graffito is when the drawing itself still remains extant. In such cases, we use published data as a starting point, but we are also able to make our own editorial decisions about the subject matter of the drawing, how to describe it, and its relation to any text that is nearby. The material with which we are working, therefore, includes a range of different information about the figural graffiti of Pompeii and Herculaneum: from brief verbal descriptions, to line-drawings, to the best case scenario when an inscription is still extant.

Several challenges arise when making decisions about how to edit and digitize figural graffiti. These can depend on how a drawing may or may not relate to a textual graffito, whether or not a drawing is extant, and how to interpret and standardize legacy data.

Three of our main methodological questions are:

1. *How to define an entry?* Where, for example, does one entry stop and another begin? Do we catalog series or clusters of graffiti as a single database entry, or separate them as individual images each with its own entry? How do we account for or represent the larger context?
2. *How to describe a drawing?* Namely, how do we represent ancient drawings with verbal descriptions? How best do we compose the Latin for the description? How much detail should be given in our description? Here, there arise issues both of standardization and of interpretation, or over-interpretation.
3. *How can we make drawings searchable?* What is the most effective way to categorize figural graffiti so that a user can search for them easily? Ideally, we would like to make it possible for users both to browse and to locate specific images.

How to define an epigraphic entry?

One of the first challenges we face in working with figural graffiti is deciding how to define an entry, that is, to consider whether or not multiple elements should be part of the same EDR record or should be given separate entries. First, we must ask: *can we be assured* that certain elements were meant to be understood together? There might be an issue of accretion or accumulation, where additional graffiti have been added subsequently. A related challenge is then, if we create individual entries for separate elements, how do we avoid losing information about the relationship among the graffiti? While from Pompeii rather than Herculaneum, this rather complicated example (Figure 8) illustrates how

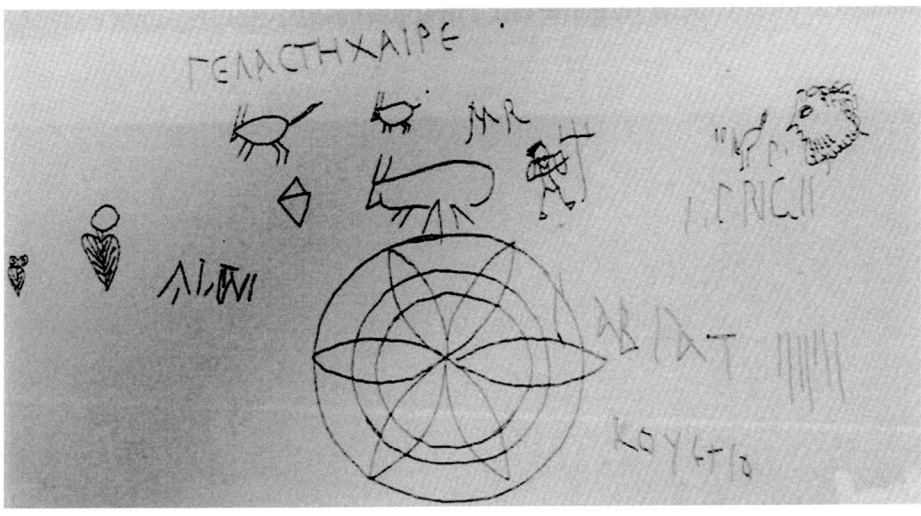

FIGURE 8. LINE-DRAWING DISPLAYING A COLLECTION OF TEXTUAL AND FIGURAL GRAFFITI (CIL, IV 8383-8386); UNPUBLISHED SKETCH OF MATTEO DELLA CORTE FROM THE ARCHIVES OF THE CORPUS INSCRIPTIONUM LATINARUM AT THE BERLIN-BRANDENBURG ACADEMY OF SCIENCE AND HUMANITIES

obscure the relationships between clusters of graffiti may be and the difficulty of determining how best to display these in a database.

Altogether, this cluster contains a total of ten different figural and six textual graffiti. A number of different images appear here, including a small gladiator with trident, a face in profile, leaves, several animals, and geometric shapes as well as the name *Atini* and the greeting Γελαστὴ χαῖρε. A grouping such as this raises many interpretive questions. What is the relationship, if any, between the figural and the textual graffiti? Or, how should that relationship be best represented? Fortunately, in this instance a sketch had been made by Matteo Della Corte, providing an overall view of the arrangement of these graffiti. The best the *Corpus* could do was to associate the various figural graffiti with nearby textual inscriptions. These sixteen separate items were therefore noted among four entries in CIL (IV 8383-8386). For this cluster, we have decided, instead, to give each element on the wall a unique identifier. First, it is not clear that the texts are clearly linked to any of the drawings. Secondly, if we create individual entries, the field for measurements in EDR permits us to give the measurements for each individual element. Thirdly, EDR has provided an additional solution to the issue of representing context via the use of hyperlinks to other nearby inscriptions.

Schedae numerus: EDR143634
Regio antiqua: LaC
Regio nostrae aetatis: I
Urbs antiqua: Herculaneum
Urbs nostrae aetatis: Ercolano (Napoli)
Locus inventionis: Ercolano (Napoli), Insula V.35, Casa del Gran Portale
Locus adservationis: Ercolano (Napoli), Insula V.35, Casa del Gran Portale
Rerum inscriptarum distributio: aedificium
Rei materia: tectorium
Mensurae: alt.: 6.70 lat.: 8.30 Crass./Diam.: 0.00 litt. alt.: ?
Status tituli: tit. integer
Scriptura: litt. scariph.
Lingua:
Titulorum distributio: cetera
Virorum distributio:
Editiones: CIL 04, 10711 (nota) (1)
M. Langner, Antike Graffitizeichnungen: Motive, Gestaltung und Bedeutung. Weisbaden 2001, n. 970 (gladiator helmet) (2)
Textus:

((:galea gladiatoria cum crista ad sin.))

Apparatus: Textus secundum (2). Beall, Bey IV, McCrory, Opdenhoff, Tomasi, et Zimmermann Damer contulerunt a. 2014.
Prope EDR143814, EDR143815, EDR143832, EDR143833, EDR144659, EDR144783, EDR144784.
Tempus: 1 d.C. / 79 d.C. (archaeologia)
Schedae scriptor: Erika DAMER **Tempus schedae:** 30-04-2015 (18-08-2015)

 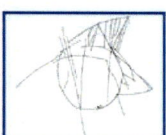 

FIGURE 9. EDR143634. EDR ENTRY FOR GLADIATORIAL HELMET IN THE CASA DEL GRAN PORTALE AT HERCULANEUM, WITH NEARBY HELMETS ASSOCIATED VIA HYPERLINKS

These hyperlinks are created by automatically when we include EDR record numbers in the apparatus field (cf. Figure 9). For groups of inscriptions, we have decided to upload a series of images to EDR, including illustrations of each graffito and the composite sketch of all graffiti, to give the context of the entire cluster and the relationship of the graffiti to each other.

We encounter clusters of graffiti associated with a single CIL entry in Herculaneum as well. Returning to the example of the alphabet from Herculaneum, mentioned previously (Figure 6), the entry for CIL, IV 10711 notes that in addition to a graffito of the alphabet, a series of nine gladiator helmets and a small phallus were also drawn on the wall. During our field season in Herculaneum in 2014, we were not successful in finding the small phallus, but we did locate the alphabet and identify six of the nine helmets.[12] Here too we have created a separate database

---

[12] Langner (2001) located eight of the helmets (n. 963-970) and noted that the ninth was lost (n. 971).

entry for each helmet (cf. EDR143634, Figure 9). By making individual records, we have a unique identifier for each image, in the form of the EDR number, so that users can cite a *specific* parallel precisely. Likewise, with separate entries for each helmet, we can record the precise measurements for each image. Yet, since separating each drawing can obscure how the images relate to one another in the group, as with the previous example, we also upload to EDR an overall image of the group of helmets together for every individual entry.

In these two cases just discussed, we are fortunate to have contextual data (a sketch providing an overview, six gladiatorial helmets still extant) that informs our understanding of how text and image may relate. More often, unfortunately, we are left with only legacy data, i.e. brief mention of a figural graffito in the apparatus of a CIL entry and given without illustration. Here, association of graffiti can be tricky. Proximity does not always indicate a relationship between text and image. Indeed, there may be no relationship at all between the figural and textual graffiti (or, in the case of the Pompeian cluster above, between figural and other figural graffiti); therefore, putting multiple graffiti in the same EDR record may suggest a relationship where none exists. Given these circumstances, we prefer to create separate EDR entries for the text and the image and to use the EDR hyperlinks to note that each is found near the other.

How to describe drawings?

A second challenge occurs when we must decide how much interpretation to offer when we describe a graffito for a database entry. When CIL has included mention of a drawing, we generally incorporate that description directly into our entry. With figural graffiti documented by Martin Langner, we must create a summary in Latin and when doing so, we attempt to give as full as possible a description of the elements of the image. With this camel (Langner 2001, n. 1443), for instance, we offer a full description in Latin that accounts for all the features of the drawing: *camelus dromedarius cum cauda, lodicem gerens, ad dextram incedens* (Figure 10).

In this example, we have followed the conventions of some figural graffiti described included in CIL by giving details such as the direction the image is facing, as well as using participles to add information about movement or other elements of the image.[13] We could, instead, offer a simpler verbal description with a list of nouns naming elements of the drawing. Here, for example, we could offer the description '*camelus et lodix*' using only nominative forms to aid textual searches. At this point, however, we have decided to provide as full a

---

[13] Cf. CIL, IV 10596 (description of figural graffito): *ad d(extram) figurae graphio delineatae, quae representat virum nixum baculo qui umero suppositus est*; IV 10600: *iuxta figuram cervi stantis*.

EAGLE ELECTRONIC ARCHIVE OF GREEK AND LATIN EPIGRAPHY
International Federation of Epigraphic Databases
under the patronage of
Association Internationale d'Épigraphie Grecque et Latine - AIEGL

Schedae numerus: EDR144514
Regio antiqua: LaC
Regio nostrae aetatis: I
Urbs antiqua: Herculaneum
Urbs nostrae aetatis: Ercolano (Napoli)
Locus inventionis: Ercolano (Napoli), Insula V.1, Casa Sannitica
Locus adservationis: Ercolano (Napoli), Insula V.1, Casa Sannitica
Rerum inscriptarum distributio: aedificium
Rei materia: tectorium
Mensurae: alt.: 21.00 lat.: 25.80 Crass./Diam.: 0.00 litt. alt.: ?
Status tituli: tit. integer
Scriptura: litt. scariph.
Lingua:
Titulorum distributio: cetera
Virorum distributio:
Editiones: M. Langner, Antike Graffitizeichnungen: Motive, Gestaltung und Bedeutung. Wiesbaden 2001, n. 1443 (Esel/camel) (1)
Textus:

((:camelus dromedarius cum cauda, lodicem gerens, ad dextram incedens))

Apparatus: Textus secundum (1), Contulerunt Beall, Bey IV, McCrory, Opdenhoff, Tomasi, Zimmermann Damer a. 2014.
Tempus: 1 d.C. / 79 d.C. (archaeologia)
Schedae scriptor: Erika DAMER **Tempus schedae:** 25-11-2014 (16-11-2015)

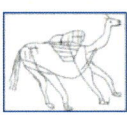

FIGURE 10. EXAMPLE OF AN ENTRY FOR A FIGURAL GRAFFITO NOT FOUND IN CIL (EDR144514)

description as possible and to provide a list of descriptive nouns in the nominative as associated 'tags' for the entry. (More on this, below.)

A second example is more colorful but equally complex. How does one identify or even begin to describe this image (Figure 11)?[14]

Our answer: through description of as many elements as possible. Here, we have the opposite challenge of, for example, the frequent images of birds found among catacomb inscriptions. There, a simple bird with few details is repeated on many inscriptions.[15] In our instance, we have an entirely uncommon image with many unusual details.[16]

---

[14] This image is available online at www.edr-edr.it (EDR145030).
[15] A search for *avis* in the Epigraphic Database Bari (http://www.edb.uniba.it/), for example, returns 1798 results (information retrieved January 12, 2016).
[16] Certain elements of this image may be modern additions. Indeed, if this were not inscribed alongside graffiti of a camel and bird that have certain ancient parallels, it would almost assuredly be classified as modern. We follow Martin Langner in cataloging it along with the other figural graffiti in the Samnite House (V.1) at Herculaneum.

FIGURE 11. FIGURAL GRAFFITO FROM HERCULANEUM (FROM LANGNER 2001: N. 1372)

As one might imagine, issues of interpretation can arise even with simple descriptions of images. In truth, we have encountered more difficulties with interpretation in the case of drawings that have been described by CIL. The first example comes from a shop in Pompeii and represents text and a drawing (CIL, IV 8185). The plaster has clearly broken off, so we do not know if this was part of a larger scene. What remains are two lines of text and one figure, which would seem to be a drawing of a person facing forward and rendered with head and shoulders. CIL describes it thus: *herma muliebris prospiciens* (Figure 12).

Is this drawing clearly depicting a female? It is difficult to argue from either the hairstyle or the clothing that the figure is female. Here, we can only assume that the editors of CIL identified the image as female because the text above mentions the female name Fortunata. But are we sure the image is meant to illustrate the text? Or that the image and text are meant to be read together? Since the figure is clearly not enacting the verb of the text, could this be either Fortunata or Antonius?

The head of a woman, described in relation to a textual graffito from the Suburban Baths in Herculaneum (Figure 13), raises similar problems with verbal descriptions of figural graffiti. In this case, CIL does not reproduce an image of the sketch; it

n. 1

8185 In huius tabernae pomariae parietis orientalis summo podio negligenter delineata est herma muliebris prospiciens, cui supra scriptus est, longitudine cm. 28

Descripsi et edidi N. S. 1912, p. 405, n. 8 cum imagine, Diehl 1021 cum adn.

Mula fella⟨a⟩t. [A]ntoni(?) / Fortunata a(eris) a(ssibus) (duobus).
Diehl legit *Mu[. . .]a fella a. II iitori.*

FIGURE 12. CIL ENTRY FOR TEXTUAL AND FIGURAL GRAFFITI (CIL, IV 8185)

only notes that the four-line inscription of CIL, IV 10676 appears below a drawing of a female (*infra mulieris imaginem*). In this instance, too, the text nearby includes two names, one female and one male. The drawing has appeared in multiple publications (Della Corte 1960, Deiss 1989, Maulucci 1993) (Figure 14).

Again, we might question whether this figure should be identified as female. At first, we were not even certain that we had located the correct apograph for the drawing. There is considerable discrepancy between the description of the drawing in CIL, IV 10676 as female and with no mention of the long nose or the other features in this line-drawing.

Another reason we suspected there might be a mistake was that Martin Langner had catalogued the drawing associated with CIL, IV 10676, describing it as a 'Phalluskopf.' He included no mention of gender and he categorized this drawing among several examples of drawings of heads with phallic features. The graffito is in a room that is sealed off, with no access, so we were unable to view it in person. Eventually, however, photographs published by Antonio Varone in his recent two-volume work[17] providing images of extant ancient graffiti allowed us

---
[17] Varone 2012: 509.

10676 Ad sin. 10675, infra mulieris imaginem graphio delineatam in spatio lato m. 0,37.
Haec imago est apographi non charta perlucida exarati, sed descripti et in ipso describendo minuti

HEΛMΓΡΟΣ ΓΥΜΝΙGENIΛΕ ΔΟΜΙΝΛΕ
VENI ΡVΤEΟΛΟΣ IN VICO ΤIΜΝΙΛΝΟ ΕΤΑVΛΕΛΕ
ΛΜΕΣΣΙΟ ΝVΜVΛΛΛΙΟ HEΛMΓΡΟΤΕΜ CHOELI

FIGURE 13. CIL, IV 10676, WITH FIGURAL GRAFFITO NOTED

FIGURE 14. APOGRAPH OF FIGURAL GRAFFITO REFERRED TO IN THE NOTE AT CIL, IV 10676 (FROM LANGNER 2001: N. 309)

to confirm that this *is* indeed the correct graffito drawing – somewhat above but also drawn partly *through* the text of CIL, IV 10676.

Neither description offered by CIL or by Langner, however, seems altogether satisfactory. There are no obvious markers of female identity and even the description of *Phalluskopf* is less than transparent. Thus this one drawing has two published descriptions that vary greatly and that each lead to a very different understanding of the graffito. What should we then do in such situations? Do we repeat the identification of CIL? Or do we offer a less specific description, merely labeling this a *hominis figura*? In the end, our solution is to offer our own description, which is more detailed but less interpretative, with an emphasis on specific features of the image that are readily identifiable: *caput acutum cum nasone longo et corona, gryllus?* (Figure 15). We note our hesitation with such identification by labeling the image: *gryllus?* ('caricature?'). We also document Langner's description and CIL's earlier identification in our entry for EDR.

The issue of interpretation arises most often in relation to identification. Other examples concern identifying the particular *types* of gladiators or the species of animals, who are assuredly quadrupeds but in some drawings could be any type of animal with four legs (stags, boars, dogs). In such cases, our solution is to describe a drawing with more generic, yet accurate, terms such as 'gladiator,' without

EAGLE ELECTRONIC ARCHIVE OF GREEK AND LATIN EPIGRAPHY
International Federation of Epigraphic Databases
under the patronage of
Association Internationale d'Épigraphie Grecque et Latine - AIEGL

Schedae numerus: EDR143636
Regio antiqua: LaC
Regio nostrae aetatis: I
Urbs antiqua: Herculaneum
Urbs nostrae aetatis: Ercolano (Napoli)
Locus inventionis: Ercolano (Napoli), Terme Suburbane
Locus adservationis: Ercolano (Napoli), Terme Suburbane
Rerum inscriptarum distributio: aedificium
Rei materia: tectorium
Mensurae: alt.: 25.00   lat.: 0.00   Crass./Diam.: 0.00   litt. alt.: ?
Status tituli: tit. integer
Scriptura: litt. scariph.
Lingua:
Titulorum distributio: cetera
Virorum distributio:
Editiones: CIL 04, 10676 (1)
M. Langner, Antike Graffitizeichnungen: Motive, Gestaltung und Bedeutung. Wiesbaden 2001, n. 309 (Phalluskopf) (2)
A. Varone, Titulorum graphio exaratorum qui in CIL Vol. IV collecti sunt imagines, Roma 2012, vol. II, p. 509 con foto (3)
Textus:

((:caput acutum cum nasone longo et corona, gryllus?))

Apparatus: Textus et mensurae secundum (2); Image identified as "mulieris imago" at (1), fortasse non recte
Tempus: 1 d.C. / 79 d.C. (archaeologia)
Schedae scriptor: REBECCA BENEFIEL (HOLLY SYPNIEWSKI)   **Tempus schedae:** 21-11-2014 (21-09-2015)

FIGURE 15. EDR143636, WITH DESCRIPTION OF FIGURAL GRAFFITO (A HEAD) INTERPRETED VARIOUSLY

further specification, or 'animal' rather than *cervus, aper*, or *canis*. Similarly, if we cannot determine male or female, we prefer to describe the drawing as something more neutral, e.g. *facies hominis*. In the AGP search engine we can then indicate possible but not certain identification with a descriptor, or tag, that comes with a question mark: e.g. 'stag?'.

How to search for drawings?

The third challenge that we face is how to create efficient search mechanisms for inscriptions that are images or text-image combinations. In the AGP search engine, we aim to complement the capabilities of EDR by providing additional ways to search for these non-textual, figural graffiti. Since we describe the content of the figural graffito in the Textus field of EDR, it is possible for a user to locate a graffito drawing. However, with text-based searching, a user would need to need to know the vocabulary used to describe the drawing. Would someone ever think to search for '*camelus*' without prior knowledge that there is a figural graffito of a camel in Herculaneum? Or, if you search for '*gladiator*,' the text field will give you results for all inscriptions that mention gladiators as well as drawings where we have described gladiators. If, however, we've described the gladiator more specifically as a '*retiarius*' or we describe specific types of gladiatorial equipment, such drawings will be omitted from the list of search results.

Building the Ancient Graffiti Project Search Engine

We are therefore designing AGP (http://agp.wlu.edu) with the capacity for locating figural graffiti through a two-prong solution: with both browsing and searching possibilities.[18]

First, we have highlighted the presence of graffiti drawings and one's ability to locate them by creating as one of the main options at the top of the screen: 'Browse All Drawings' (Figure 16).

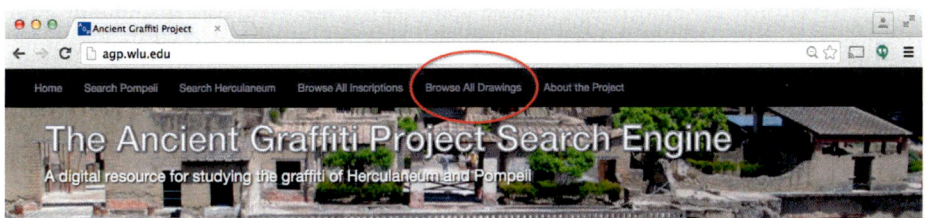

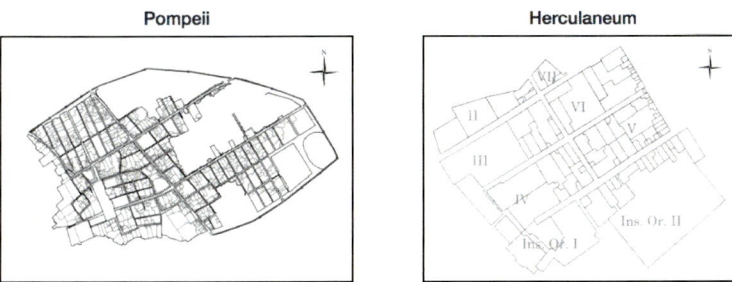

FIGURE 16. LAUNCH PAD OF THE ANCIENT GRAFFITI PROJECT SEARCH ENGINE

'Browse All Drawings' returns all figural graffiti processed by AGP so far, from both Pompeii and Herculaneum. One can then choose to limit the results by using the filters on the left hand side of the page. So, for example, to find figural graffiti only from Herculaneum, a user would click the arrow for 'City,' then check the box for 'Herculaneum,' and then click at the top of the filters list the box 'Refine Results' (Figure 17). To limit the results to a particular building, a user could click the arrow for 'Property,' then choose the City, Regio/Insula, and Property, *or* simply click on the highlighted address and limit the results to that particular building. It is possible to use the filters to limit results in several other ways as well.

---

[18] Many thanks go to Professor Sara Sprenkle and her computer science students, especially Jamie White, at Washington and Lee University who have been building the website.

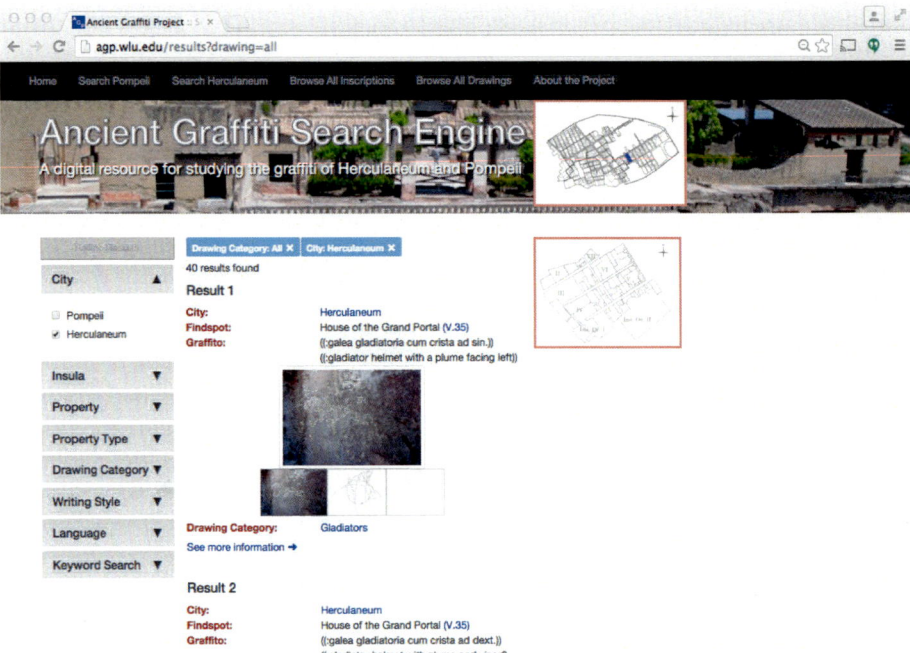

FIGURE 17. FIGURAL GRAFFITI RESULTS, ONLY FROM HERCULANEUM

We have also defined nine broad categories for figural graffiti (Drawing Category) to allow a user to conduct a search by subject matter. These together cover all the types of figural graffiti we have encountered so far. They are, in alphabetical order: animals, boats, erotic images, geometric designs, gladiators, human figures, other, and plants (Figure 18). A drawing that includes both human figures and animals, for example a person leading an animal by a leash, is retrieved in both categories.

Choosing a category will return all examples in that category. So, for example, the category of 'Gladiators' will return sketches of individual gladiators, gladiators fighting in pairs, and gladiatorial equipment such as helmets. 'Geometric designs' includes the popular image of compass-drawn circles as well as other triangles, squares, and simple shapes. As we process greater numbers of figural graffiti, the number of results returned for these categories will become larger.

As mentioned, we are developing a method of filters and tags that will allow a user to move beyond browsing. These filters will allow a user 1) to limit an initial return of results, 2) to retrieve more specific results, or 3) to perform a secondary level of search. It will certainly be helpful to refine results of an entire category to include only a subset of that category, for example, only pairs of gladiators instead of all gladiators and their equipment.

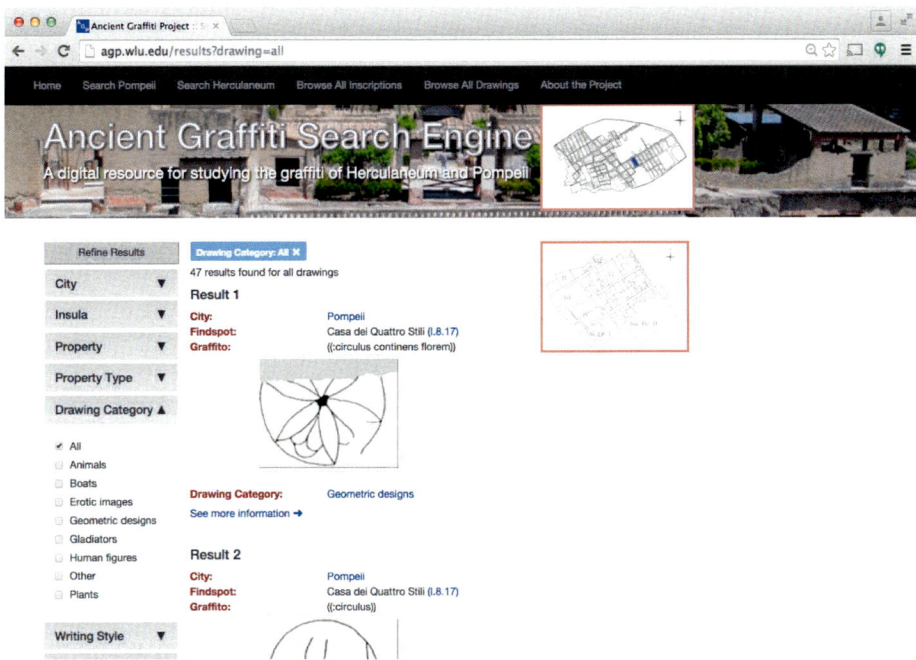

FIGURE 18. AGP DRAWING CATEGORY OPTIONS FOR RETRIEVING FIGURAL GRAFFITI

At present, the Drawing Category works as both a Category and as a 'tag.' Within a list of results, if a user clicks on that definition, e.g. Animals, the list then shifts to displaying all graffiti associated with the Drawing Category of 'Animals.' We will be creating a fuller list of tags to apply to figural graffiti and allow for greater specificity of searching. By using tags, we can also assign multiple terms to a single image, e.g. stag and dog (for a drawing that includes the two animals together). Our goal is ultimately to enable searches by these tags as well, so a user can directly find all drawings with dogs. The search capacity will allow a user to search the tags or the Latin description, so both *navis* and 'boat' will return hits. Again, standardization is necessary. We are currently developing a list of tags that is comprehensive and flexible enough to cover all graffiti, but that includes a level of standardization so that the list of tags offers extensible terms. A list of sample potential tags includes:

> Animal types: horse, boar, dog, stag
> Geometric shapes: triangle, circle, square, quadrangle
> Boats: rudder, net, hull, oars, mast
> Equipment: helmet, greaves, net, shield, sword, net, trident
> Architecture: column, column base, ladder

The system of filters will work in conjunction with these tags, and will allow a user to refine his or her search, to limit an initial list of results, to move directly to a desired graffito, or to create a combination of search parameters. So, a user will be able to do a broad search for all drawings of animals, and then filter to limit the results to find what kind of animals are drawn in taverns, for example, but not public buildings or houses.

This system of tags and filters is in the early stages of development. These are our proposed solutions for confronting the challenges of working with text and image, and our ideas for creating a resource to complement the strengths of EDR with search capabilities for characteristics that are specific to these heterogeneous, individualized handwritten inscriptions.

Bibliography

CIL IV. *Corpus Inscriptionum Latinarum*, vol. IV, published 1871; Supplementi pars I, published 1898; Supplementi pars II, published 1909; Supplementi pars III (fasc. I-IV), published 1952-1970; Supplementi pars IV, published 2011.

Cooley, A. E. and Cooley M. G. L. 2014. *Pompeii and Herculaneum: A Sourcebook*. 2nd ed. London and New York, Routledge.

Deiss, J. J. 1989. *Herculaneum: Italy's Buried Treasure*. Malibu, J. Paul Getty Museum.

Della Corte, M. 1958. Le iscrizioni di Ercolano. *Rendiconti della Accademia di Archeologia Lettere e Belle Arti (Napoli)* 33: 239-308.

Della Corte, M. 1960. *Loves and Lovers in Ancient Pompeii, a Pompeian erotic anthology*. Translated by A. W. Van Buren. Cava dei Tirreni, di Mauro.

Garrucci, R. 1856. *Graffiti de Pompéi: inscriptions et gravures tracées au stylet*, 2nd ed. Paris, Duprat.

Guadagno, G. 1983. Herculanensium Augustalium Aedes. *Cronache Ercolanesi* 13: 159-175.

Guadagno, G. 1988. I graffiti della Aedes Augustalium: documenti sull'accesso all'Augustalità. *Cronache Ercolanesi* 18: 199-204.

Guidobaldi, M. P. and Esposito, D. 2012. *Ercolano. Colori di una città sepolta*. Verona, Arsenale.

Langner, M. 2001. *Antike Graffitizeichnungen: Motive, Gestaltung und Bedeutung, Palilia, 11*. Wiesbaden, L. Reichert.

Maulucci Vivolo, F. P. 1993. *Pompei. I graffiti figurati*. Foggia, Bastogi.

Tan Timh, T. 1988. *La Casa dei Cervi a Herculanum*. Roma, Giorgio Bretschneider.

Varone, A. 2000. Spigolature epigrafiche ercolanesi. *Rivista di Studi Pompeiani* 11: 276-281.

Varone, A. 2012. *Titulorum Graphio Exaratorum qui in C.I.L. Volume IV collecti sunt. Imagines I-II*. Roma, L'Erma di Bretschneider.

Wallace-Hadrill, A. 2011. *Herculaneum: Past and Future*. London, Frances Lincoln.

Is still Arabia at the margins of digital Epigraphy? Challenges in the digitization of the pre-Islamic inscriptions in the project DASI.

Alessandra Avanzini[*], Annamaria De Santis[**],
Daniele Marotta[**] and Irene Rossi[**]
Digital Archive for the Study of pre-Islamic Arabian Inscriptions
[*]University of Pisa and [**] Scuola Normale Superiore, Pisa

DASI: overview of the project

Since the late 2nd millennium BC until the expansion of Islam, Arabia produced an enormous amount of inscriptions in different languages and scripts (Macdonald 2000). This epigraphic heritage is still poorly known outside the scientific community studying the Semitic languages or the history of the Arabian Peninsula. Collecting and digitizing those inscriptions is of fundamental importance for the Arabian studies, since they are the only direct written sources that the pre-Islamic Arabian civilizations have left, but it is equally important in the frame of digital epigraphy, for the challenges that these documents lead to face.

DASI – Digital Archive for the study of pre-Islamic Arabian inscriptions is an ERC Advanced Grant project (2011-2016) of the University of Pisa, in collaboration with Scuola Normale Superiore of Pisa, that aims at getting the whole corpus of ancient Arabian inscriptions inventoried and digitized, to enhance historic and cultural knowledge of Ancient Arabia and strengthen the linguistic study of texts.[1]

Presently, the archive includes about 9000 inscriptions, nearly 7700 of which are already published in the online open archive (http://dasi.humnet.unipi.it). The majority of DASI texts are in the Ancient South Arabian languages, but, thanks to a partnership with the UMR Orient et Méditerranée of the CNRS-Paris and with the project *OCIANA-The Online Corpus of the Inscriptions of Ancient North Arabia* of the University of Oxford, a number of inscriptions in the Aramaic and Ancient North Arabian languages have enriched the archive.

In the present contribution, the focus is on the Ancient South Arabian (ASA) corpus, for two reasons: first, it provides enough material to reflect on specific

---

[1] The research leading to the results presented in this paper has received funding from the European Research Council under the European Union's Seventh Framework Programme (FP7/2007-2013)/ERC grant agreement n° 269774.

Figure 1. Minaic inscription MṢM 3645 from the Military Museum of Ṣanʿāʾ (image DASI by permission of General Organization of Antiquities and Museums, Yemen)

digitization issues, as it is the largest corpus in DASI; second, this collection is the result of 15 years of work, during which the principles and the guidelines of the digitization process have evolved, as we will see later on.

Ancient South Arabian epigraphy: introduction to the subject

The Ancient South Arabian corpus attests four main Semitic languages, which are identifiable from the lexical and, especially, the morphological point of view: they are the Sabaic, the Minaic, the Qatabanic and the Hadramitic – expression of the four main kingdoms which flourished in the region of modern Yemen since the 1st millennium BC (Stein 2011). 'Public' (or 'monumental') inscriptions were recorded on various supports: outcrops of natural rocks, monumental structures and a variety of objects for funerary, cultic, votive but also domestic use such as plaques, stelae, incense burners, statues and figurines, altars, containers, personal ornaments etc. Besides the record of worship acts (like pilgrimages or sacred hunts) or simple onomastic inscriptions, such as those on tombs and funerary objects, the main typologies of inscriptions are dedications to the deities, celebrations of building activities, and legal regulations. A further category of texts is represented by graffiti, texts of extemporary nature, usually drawn or engraved on rocks or walls, and generally recording names. Rarely some texts with a narrative character, or a digression, are found and no literary text is known so far.

A very geometric and regular monumental writing is attested since the 9th–8th century BC to write down the 'public' inscriptions. Each letter is graphically separated from the adjacent ones and the division between the words is marked by a vertical trait. Being a Semitic script, the South Arabian *ductus* of writing is normally right-to-left. However, in the first half of the 1st millennium BC, the importance of the kingdom of Sabaʾ, which used a boustrophedon *ductus*, influenced the style of some inscriptions of the other kingdoms. Apart from regional variations, the writing style followed a quite uniform evolution from more geometric to more ornate shapes of the letters in the whole of South Arabia, during the long history of its civilization. The writing technique also changed from carving the letters on the stone to sculpting the surface around them, to obtain a text in relief.

In the years 1970s, a new typology of writing of the South Arabian alphabet was discovered. Incised with a stylus or sometimes painted on wooden sticks and palm leaves' stalks, the letters have a less geometric shape. This cursive (or minuscule) writing was in use since the end of the 2nd millennium BC to record private and movable documents, like letters and contracts.

A step forward from CSAI: semi-structured or structured information?

The first attempt to a mass digitization of the South Arabian epigraphic heritage was the project *CSAI – Corpus of South Arabian Inscriptions*, which had been set up in 2001 by the same research group of the University of Pisa. The digital edition of the inscriptions consisted of XML files, each one grouping the inscriptions belonging to one ASA sub-corpus. The description model focused on the text, whose editorial interventions and onomastic features were marked. As DASI is the successor of CSAI, it has inherited this experience, which however has proven to be obsolete, both in the description model and in the technical infrastructure. Therefore, the first challenge for DASI was to update and make them aligned with those currently in use in digital epigraphy.

DASI is a hybrid system that combines both the database and the XML approach to archive and display data. The database stores not only metadata, but also texts encoded in XML format, being the data entry provided with an editing module specifically developed to encode pre-Islamic Arabian inscriptions. In particular, the text of the inscriptions is indexed in order to perform complex full-text queries, such as textual variants, word ranges etc.

Each item digitized in DASI is described as a physical object connected to one or more epigraphs, each one provided with its own images and bibliography. The dual nature of inscribed artefacts is represented by two separate but strictly related entities: 'Epigraph' and 'Object'.[2]

Information about a support is not embedded in the attributes of the 'Epigraph', but the entity 'Object' has its own attributes regarding: type of support, materials and dimensions, deposit and archaeological context, and the detailed description of its decorative elements. Contextual entities are also considered such as 'Site', that provides information about provenance or place of production: ancient and modern toponyms, geographical coordinates, country, region, ancient kingdom, archaeological information about the sites, such as monuments, history of studies, archaeological missions etc.

Text encoding: the alignment to a standard

The 'Epigraph' entity provides, with its attributes, information on: linguistic features, writing, chronology, type of text, notes of apparatus, general and cultural notes.

---

[2] The characteristics of the system, the data model and the search tools of the public website are extensively described in Avanzini et al. 2014.

The XML editor integrated into the data entry allows to encode and archive the text directly in XML format without knowing XML syntax (Figure 2). The Latin transliteration (UTF-8 set) is entered and a set of tags, that represent specific phenomena defined within the project, are selected from menus of buttons.

The editor ensures that XML documents are valid and well-formed, by preventing users from entering elements in positions not allowed by the EpiDoc schema and not considered within the project. Moreover it verifies, by fragmentation, that tags are rightly nested in order to avoid overlapping.

DASI has decided to encode:

- structural phenomena: line breaks and in-word line breaks;
- non structural text parts, such as phenomena concerning the relationship between text and support: broken support, change of support and turn of side;
- transcription phenomena: clitic components, uncertain reading, gaps, illegible or lost lines of text;
- editorial interventions: supplied text (restoration in lacuna), supplement of omitted characters, superfluous characters, corrections of the editor, reading or interpretation variants;
- onomastics: names of individuals and social groups, toponyms, etc.;
- textual portions: signatures, eponyms, etc.;
- symbols such as word dividers, geometric signatures and paraphs.

The tags included in the text codified by CSAI and imported into DASI, have been mapped to be compliant with EpiDoc (8.21 version). However some uses of the EpiDoc elements are peculiar to the project, and distance themselves from the EpiDoc Guidelines (Elliott *et al.* 2007-2014).[3]

Given that the domain of application of EpiDoc has been for a long time only Greek and Latin epigraphy, different styles of encoding have been created in DASI, on the basis of the editorial tradition of the research field, in order to meet the objectives of the project and the specific needs of the Semitic languages.

1) Transcription phenomena

According to the EpiDoc Guidelines, the text direction, and its possible changes, should be expressed within the element <*lb/*>, that introduces the lines of text encoded. Since one direction - right-to-left, bustrophedon or left-to-right *cursus* - is uniformly attested in each inscription of DASI, this information is included

---

[3] Such a situation is not new in the EpiDoc community, as it is evidenced by the presence of the sections 'Externally maintained guidelines for specialized communities' and 'Correspondences between EpiDoc and other community guidelines' in the EpiDoc Guidelines.

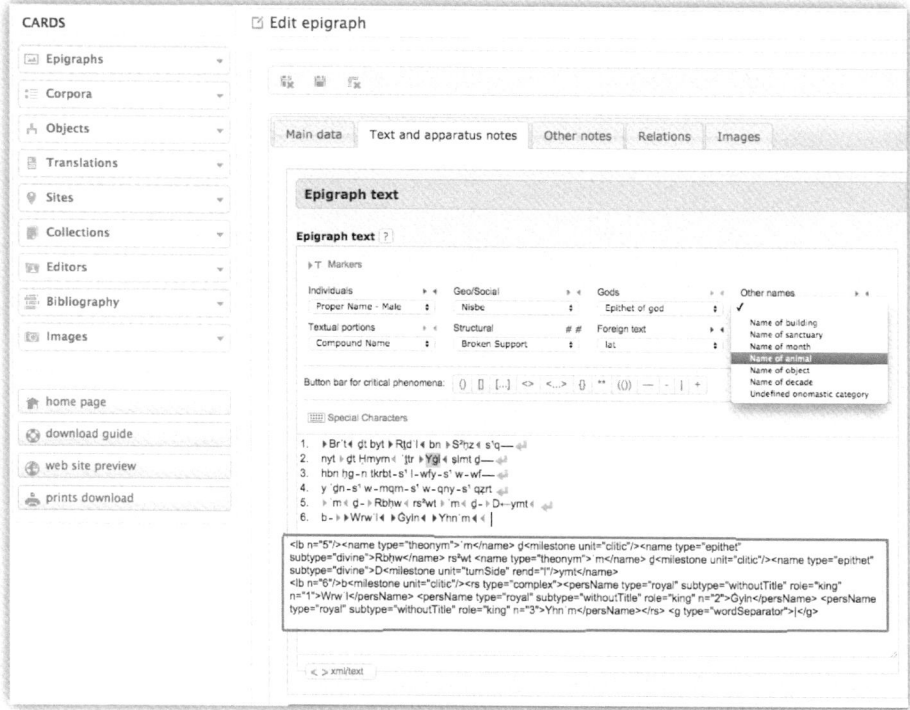

FIGURE 2. EDITOR OF THE 'EPIGRAPH' WITH EXAMPLE OF TEXT ENCODING.

among the metadata of the entire inscription. It is therefore encoded in the section *//layoutDesc/layout/* (see further on 'Exposing the EpiDoc files').

2) Editorial interventions

There are two main differences related to representation and encoding. The case of the uncertain reading is emblematic of the differences in representation (Figure 3): this phenomenon could not be represented with a dot under the uncertain characters, as dot is used as a diacritical mark to transcribe some phonemes typical of the Semitic languages (e.g. letter ḍ which transcribes the dental emphatic phoneme).

Moreover, whereas the EpiDoc Guidelines suggest to choose whether to encode critical interventions within the text or to add them outside, in a specific section, DASI employs both the approaches. If a reading or interpretation variant of a word/textual portion has the same probability of being true as the word/text chosen as the main one, it is marked in the inline apparatus – using the *<app>*, *<lem>*, *<rdg>* elements – thus allowing to retrieve both the reading or interpretation variants, through the textual search tool, in the same context, e.g.:

Phenomena	DASI	EpiDoc		
		K-P	SEG	Leiden+
Uncertain reading	( )	aḅ	aḅ	aḅ
Illegible text	[.], [..], [...], [....], [... ...]	+++ [n. of characters, three in this case]	... [n. of characters, three in this case]	.3 [n. of characters, three in this case]
Lacuna (lines)	[... ...]	[- - - - - -] - - - - - -		lost1lin. lost?lin.
Correction of editor	*ab*	⌊ab⌋	<ab>	<:ab| orr|ba:>

FIGURE 3. REPRESENTATION OF THE EDITORIAL INTERVENTIONS IN DASI AND IN THE MAIN SYSTEMS OF REPRESENTATION ENVISAGED BY EPIDOC.

b-mlk((ml'))((mr'))-hw

b<milestone unit='clitic'/><app>
    <lem>mlk</lem>
    <rdg>ml'</rdg>
    <rdg>mr'</rdg>
</app><milestone unit='clitic'/>hw

On the other hand, several types of *apparatus criticus*, pertaining to epigraphs and their translations, such as the comments on the editorial intervention of previous editors of the text, are set apart (see below).

3) Onomastics

DASI has a marked linguistic interest for onomastics. The onomastic categories encoded in DASI are more numerous than those envisaged by EpiDoc (Figure 4). For these categories the element <*orgName*> is used (TEI P5 2015).

But differences are also present in the use of the element <*persName*>. Whereas EpiDoc has a focus on prosopography,[4] DASI focuses on the lexicographic aspect of names. Therefore the element <*persName*> does not enclose the textual portion that identifies an individual, but each single name of an individual.

Onomastics consisting of several units are enclosed by the <*rs*> element, e.g.:

---

[4] 'Personal names and prosopographical links' in Elliott et al. 2007-2014.

Onomastics	
Phoenomena	**EpiDoc Element**
Theonym	`<name type="theonym"></name>`
Epithet of god	`<name type="epithet" subtype="divine"></name>`
Name of member of royal family - male	`<persName type="royal" subtype="m" role="member"></persName>`
Name of member of royal family - female	`<persName type="royal" subtype="f" role="member"></persName>`
Name of member of royal family - unknown	`<persName type="royal" subtype="u" role="member"></persName>`
Name of the king with royal title	`<persName type="royal" subtype="withTitle" role="king"></persName>`
Name of the king without royal title	`<persName type="royal" subtype="withoutTitle" role="king"></persName>`
Name of the queen with royal title	`<persName type="royal" subtype="withTitle" role="queen"></persName>`
Name of the queen without royal title	`<persName type="royal" subtype="withoutTitle" role="queen"></persName>`
Proper name of persons	`<persName type="gender" subtype="m | f | u"></persName>`
Patronymic	`<persName type="patronymic"></persName>`
Matronymic	`<persName type="matronymic"></persName>`
Name of member of royal family patronymic	`<persName type="patronymic" subtype="royal" role="member"></persName>`
Name of member of royal family matronymic	`<persName type="matronymic" subtype="royal" role="member"></persName>`
Name of the king with royal title patronymic	`<persName type="patronymic" subtype="royalWithTitle" role="king"></persName>`
Name of the queen with royal title matronymic	`<persName type="matronymic" subtype="royalWithTitle" role="queen"></persName>`
Name of lineage name group	`<orgName type="group"></orgName>`
Name of tribe	`<orgName type="tribe"></orgName>`
Nisbe	`<rs type="nisbe"></rs>`
Name of building	`<placeName type="building"></placeName>`
Name of sanctuary	`<placeName type="sanctuary"></placeName>`
Toponym	`<placeName><placeName>`
Name of month	`<rs type="month"></rs>`
Name of decade	`<rs type="decade"></rs>`
Name of animal	`<rs type="animal"></rs>`
Name of object	`<rs type="object"></rs>`
Undefined onomastic category	`<rs type="undefinedCategory"></rs>`

FIGURE 4. ONOMASTIC ELEMENTS AND RELATED TAGS USED BY DASI.

```
<rs type='eponym'>
   <persName type='gender' subtype='m'>
      Tbʿkrb
   </persName> bn
   <persName type="patronymic">
       Mʿdkrb
   </persName> bn
   <orgName type='group'>
      Ḥzfrm
   </orgName>
</rs>
```

that has *@type* attribute, with values: eponyms, nominal groups, genealogies, compound name.

The still limited knowledge of pre-Islamic Arabian prosopography calls for this detailed analysis of the onomastic phenomena.

4) Monograms

The nature of monograms in relation to the encoding of texts is still uncertain. Monograms appear as combinations of letters forming symbolic representations of names, accompanying the texts or on supports without linear inscriptions. They are not abbreviations inside the text but rather a combination of signs decorating the objects. Often the name the monogram refers to is unknown, because some letters can be omitted in this symbolic representation or incorporated into the shape of other letters, and there may be no way to reconstruct their correct order. For these reasons DASI presently inserts monograms in the area of description as following: *//decoNote/note[@type='figurativeSubjects']/rs[@type='monogram']*.

Exposing the EpiDoc files

Although only the text is natively encoded in XML, the entire description of the epigraphs is available in the same format. Indeed a repository allows service providers using OAI-PMH protocol to harvest DASI records, which have been mapped to several standards and data models: DC, EDM and EpiDoc.[5]

The description of the epigraphs is structured in the different entities of the database, but the entity Epigraph is the pivot of the EpiDoc record. The centrality of the text, derived to EpiDoc from TEI (Text Encoding Initiative), is gained by quoting only the identifiers of the instances of the 'Epigraph', not those of the other entities, above all 'Object'. The univocal identifier of the inscription is placed in the element *//publicationStmt/idno*. In the area *//fileDesc/titleStmt/* the title and the editor of the inscription, but also of the 'Object' and 'Translation', are inserted.

As in the case of the encoding of the text, DASI has used some of the EpiDoc elements in a flexible way to better express the scientific criteria of the project and of its domain.

5) Type of text

The EpiDoc Guidelines envisage three different ways of encoding the information related to the type of text:

- *rs[@type='textType']* within the text;
- the elemet *<seg>* in *//msContents/summary*;
- the element *<term>* in *//textClass/keywords*.

It seems that the types of text are assigned on the basis of keywords and concepts referred into the texts.

---

[5] DASI records in EpiDoc format are available at http://dasi.humnet.unipi.it/de/cgi-bin/dasi-oai-x.pl?verb=ListRecords&metadataPrefix=epidoc&set=epi_set. Presently the records exposed are those pertaining to the Ancient South Arabian corpus, that can be considered the bulk of the content of the archive.

The textual typologies identified in DASI are however characterized by formulary patterns, that are composed of constituent parts (lexicon items – in particular the main verb – and morpho-syntactic features), and their linear layout. These vary diachronically but also by geographic, cultural and political area, thus indicating the existence of proper writing traditions.

Therefore, DASI uses the attribute *@type* 'textualTypology' in place of 'textType' in the area *//handDesc/handNote/rs[@type='textualTypology']* in order to point out this different perspective.

6) Critical apparatus

EpiDoc acknowledges only the *apparatus criticus* of the epigraphs. Instead, since the translation in DASI can be provided with its own critical apparatus, the section *//div[@type='apparatus']/listApp/* has been integrated with the attribute *@subtype* whose value is 'translation'. If more than one translation are linked to the epigraph, the attributes *@xml:id*, in the *<div>* of the translations, and *@corresp*, in the *<div>* of the apparatus, are added.

7) Description of the support

Multilevel vocabularies provide information about types and decoration of the supports in DASI. They have been mapped to the most common terminologies,[6] which are referred in the records exposed in DC and EDM formats.

All the levels of the vocabularies are exported in the EpiDoc files, by using only one *<objectType>* and one *<rs>*. Their values are organized according to the syntax: L1 » L2 » L3 for the support type and L1 » L2 for the type of decoration, in the sections *//support/objectType* and *//decoDesc/rs*, respectively.

8) Period

As recommended by the Guidelines, the history of the epigraphs is enclosed by the elements *<placeName>* and *<seg>* in the sections *//history/origin/origPlace/* and *//history/provenance/*.

Notwithstanding the progress of studies on Ancient Arabia, it is often difficult to attribute absolute dates to inscriptions. Each of them, if possible, is assigned to a period, identified by letters of the alphabet, whose chronological extremes are neither exact nor definitively identified.

---

[6] Getty AAT http://vocab.getty.edu, EAGLE vocabularies http://www.eagle-network.eu/resources/vocabularies/, Heritage data http://www.heritagedata.org/live/getAllSchemes.php.

Textual portions	
Phoenomena	**EpiDoc elements**
Eponym	`<rs type="eponym"></rs>`
Compound name	`<rs type="complex"></rs>`
Nominal group	`<rs type="nominalGroup"></rs>`
Genealogies	`<rs type="genealogies"></rs>`
Signature	`<seg type="signature"></seg>`
Narrative section	`<seg type="narrativeSection"></seg>`
Prayer	`<seg type="prayer"></seg>`
Foreign text	`<foreign xml:lang="..."></foreign>`

FIGURE 5. TEXTUAL PORTIONS AND RELATED TAGS USED BY DASI.

As for Ancient South Arabia, some major periods have been identified (A, B, C, D, E) which can be applied to a common periodization of the various cultural-political but also linguistic areas of the region, and are mainly defined on the basis of the historical relations among them (e.g. period A roughly covers the first half of the 1st millennium BC, characterized by the predominance of the kingdom of Saba'). However, the absolute chronological limits of these periods can shift area by area on the basis of internal features, being mainly defined by major changes or ruptures.

Considering this state of the art, the attribute *@period* of the elements *<origPlace>* and *<provenance>* has been adopted to map DASI periods. Moreover periods are explained in the section *//textClass/keywords*.

Further interpretations of the EpiDoc standard are needed in relation to the modelling of data. Some of the features of the DASI data model have been partially influenced by CSAI, before the initiatives on text encoding established proper standards.

9) Deposit

The element *<msIdentifier>* in *//msDesc/msIdentifier* indicates alternative inventory numbers, according to the EpiDoc Guidelines. Instead the element *<msPart>* is suggested for the link between an epigraph and multiple deposits.

Since DASI does not identify and describe each single fragment of the epigraph, but the whole text, the EpiDoc record identifies the entire epigraph in *//msDesc/*

msIdentifier. This is related to as many <*msPart*> as the fragments, each one provided with its own <*msIdentifier*>, through the attribute @*corresp*, in order to point out that the description refers to fragments preserved in several deposits.

10) Measures

DASI uses the element <*measureGrp*> in place of <*dimensions*>, since the three dimensions are not registered separately, but through a string of free text.

DASI Lexicon for linguistic study

As the orthographic units are not marked in the transcription, the process of tokenization is carried out in the phase of extraction. It is based on rules that consider, as the elements that distinguish one word from another, spaces and tags, in turn indicating: divider symbols (<*g type='wordSeparator'/*>), geometric signature (<*g type='paraph'*>), line breaks (<*lb n='n'/*>) and clitic components (<*milestone unit='clitic'/*>). The clitic is used to mark the separation of the different PoS that occur in a single orthographic unit. Lists of words in alphabetical order, deprived of onomastics, are thus created. These lists of words are at the basis of a new tool developed within DASI for linguistic studies which is a digital lexicon of the archived texts (Avanzini *et al.*, in press).

In fact, the history of studies of the languages of pre-Islamic Arabia is very recent compared to the important tradition of research on other Semitic languages. As the Ancient Arabian languages are fragmentarily attested only through inscriptions, the epigraphic study of the continuously growing amount of documents is the basis for the improvement of the few existing dictionaries and grammars.

DASI Lexicon avoids the XML encoding of the grammatical and lexicographic information directly on the texts, precisely because the study of the semantic and morphological characteristics of the words is still in progress, with a high level of unclearness or uncertainty.

Moreover, the preliminary annotation of the lexical items in a specific tool is particularly effective in the frame of epigraphic studies, given the high number of stereotypical texts: by assigning at one time the same semantic and grammatical analysis to multiple occurrences of a lexical item, it allows to complete the lexicographic work in a reasonable lapse of time.

The Lexicon tool includes several entities: *root, word, word form* and *occurrence*. Each *word form* – intended as a sequence of characters separated by other sequences and corresponding to the items of the word lists – is linked to one or more *occurrences*. One or more rows of translation are in turn linked to each occurrence. *Word forms*

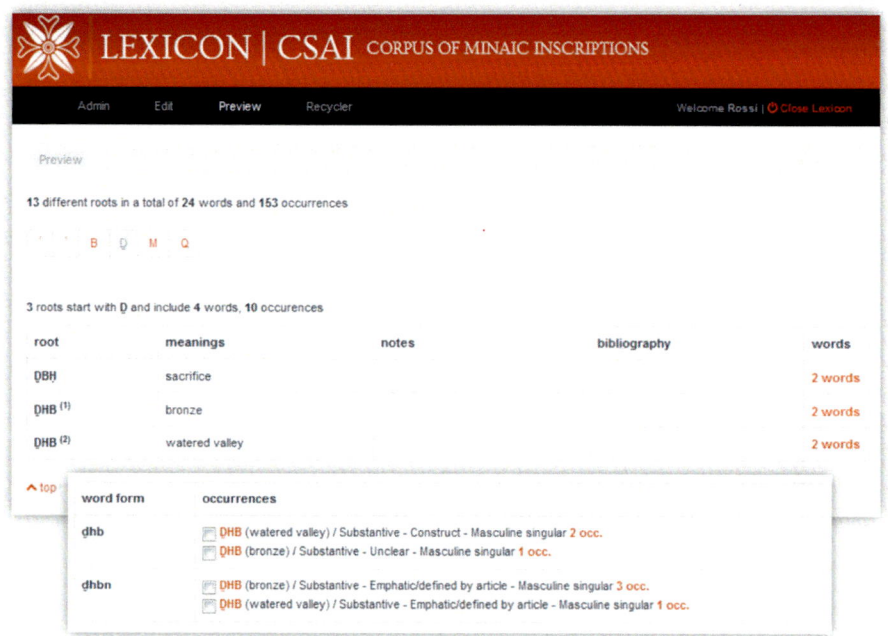

FIGURE 6. LEXICON OF THE MINAIC CORPUS: ENTITIES AND THEIR RELATIONS.

can be assigned, individually or in groups, to a *root*. While assigning a root, users attribute morphological and PoS analysis to the word form. The set of root, word form and analysis identifies a *word*. The word, not the lemma, is the intermediate level between the orthographic unit and the root, as in the other Semitic languages. Potential notes and bibliographical references complete the description of the entities (Figure 6).

The manual approach is due to several reasons. Besides sharing with the other Semitic languages a complex and ambiguous morphology that still poses challenges to computational approaches (Wintner 2014), a specific difficulty in the study of pre-Islamic Arabian languages is the exclusively epigraphic nature of the sources. The annotated corpora are not so large-scaled to drive automatic lexical acquisition, given the formulaic contexts of the inscriptions. On the other hand, the high number of *hapax legomena* causes data sparsity.

Once the lexicon concerning a single corpus is completed and synchronized with texts, it will be possible to perform advanced searches and to attempt an automatic word extractor and a morphological analyzer.

Bibliography

Avanzini, A., De Santis, A., Gallo, M., Marotta, D. and Rossi, I. (in press). Computational lexicography and digital epigraphy. Building digital lexica of fragmentary attested languages in the project DASI. In *Proceedings of the 2nd International Congress on Digital Heritage 2015* (Granada, 28th September–1st October 2015).

Avanzini, A., De Santis, A., Marotta, D. and Rossi, I. 2014. Between harmonization and peculiarities of scientific domains. Digitizing the epigraphic heritage of pre-Islamic Arabia in the project DASI. In S. Orlandi, R. Santucci, V. Casarosa and P. M. Liuzzo (eds), *Information Technologies for Epigraphy and Cultural Heritage. Proceedings of the First EAGLE International Conference*: 69-93. Roma, Sapienza Università Editrice.

DC 2012. Dublin Core Metadata Initiative – Terms. http://dublincore.org/documents/2012/06/14/dcmi-terms/

EDM 2012. Europeana Data Model. Version 5.2.3. http://pro.europeana.eu/page/edm-documentation/

Elliott, T., Bodard, G., Mylonas, E., Stoyanova, S., Tupman, C., Vanderbilt, S. *et al.* 2007-2014. *EpiDoc Guidelines: Ancient documents in TEI XML*. Version 8.21. http://www.stoa.org/epidoc/gl/latest/

Krummrey, H. and Panciera, S. (1980). Criteri di edizione e segni diacritici. *Tituli* 2: 205-215.

Macdonald, M. C. A. 2000. Reflections on the linguistic map of pre-Islamic Arabia, *Arabian Archaeology and Epigraphy* 11: 28-79.

OAI. Open Archives Initiative Protocol for Metadata Harvesting. Version 2.0. https://www.openarchives.org/pmh/

Stein, P. 2011. Ancient South Arabian, in S. Weninger (ed.). *The Semitic Languages: An International Handbook (Handbücher zur Sprach- und Kommunikationswissenschaft 36)*. Berlin and Boston, Walter de Gruyter GmbH & Co. KG.

TEI P5 2015. *Guidelines for Electronic Text Encoding and Interchange*. Version 2.9.1. http://www.tei-c.org/release/doc/tei-p5-doc/en/html/index.html

Wintner, S. 2014. Morphological processing of Semitic languages. In I. Zitouni (ed.), *Natural language processing of Semitic languages*: 43-66. Berlin, Springer.

From *Officina Lapidaria* to D.I.Y.
Encoding inscriptions from the Christian Roman Catacombs

Anita Rocco
Epigraphic Database Bari – University of Bari 'Aldo Moro'

The challenge of encoding ancient inscriptions commissioned by Christians from Rome dates back to the 1980s, when Carlo Carletti started a pioneering project of digitization[1] of the entries of the corpus of *Inscriptiones Christianae Vrbis Romae, nova series*.[2] The project, that started with a very simple program in MS-DOS intended for internal use, has turned in the last 30 years into an online database freely accessible, the Epigraphic Database Bari (EDB), one of the main content provider of the *Europeana network of Ancient Greek and Latin Epigraphy* (EAGLE), with more than 40000 records of Roman inscriptions by Christians, dating back between the third and the eighth century.

The corpus counts a huge quantity of known documents, even if obviously the numeric data are partial - depending from vagaries of preservation, accidents in discovery, completeness of publication and more unavoidable limitation factors - and don't allow us to reconstruct the real dimension of the epigraphic practice in this period, that still remain unexplored under several aspects.

The vast majority of the records consists of funerary private epitaphs from the Catacombs, the wide underground collective cemeteries of the Roman suburbs, used by Christian since the end of the third century, that could be defined the largest archive of late antique epigraphic documents known.

An archaeological approach to inscriptions, according to the most recent advances in epigraphic studies (Manacorda 2000) is behind the concept of EDB since its beginning and requires not only the analysis of the original position and of the function of each epigraphic monument, but even the reconstruction of its manufacturing process.

---

[1] For the history and the characteristics of the project see Carletti 1994 and 1997; Felle 1997, 2012 and 2014; Rocco 2015 and 2016.

[2] The ICVR Corpus started in 1922 by A. Silvagni, was published, mostly, by A. Ferrua, later supported by D. Mazzoleni and C. Carletti, between 1956 and 1992. Pursuing the work of G.B. de Rossi of the mid-1800s (IC), ICVR registers the inscriptions by Christians found in the suburban area of Rome, sorted in topographic order by consular road, then by every Catacomb. Inscriptions found inside the urban walls or the recently discovered suburban ones aren't yet included in the ICVR volumes.

An inscribed find, infact, has to be considered as a unique and original artifact of an archaeological nature. Its uniqueness lies in the fact that the epigraphic production, even if the text-bearing objects are standard and serial, releases items made original by the specific demand of the customer.

Reconstructing the physical structure and the organization of the work of an *officina lapidaria* is a very hard endeavor, lacking archaeological evidence of a defined and recognizable process plant and of the standard equipment of instruments, moreover, completely similar to those used by every marble worker.[3] An extraordinary exception in this respect comes from the two *tabernae* in the porch outside the Roman theater of Ostia, built in the age of Commodus and active until the 4th century, recently restudied by Buonopane (2012). (Figure 1)

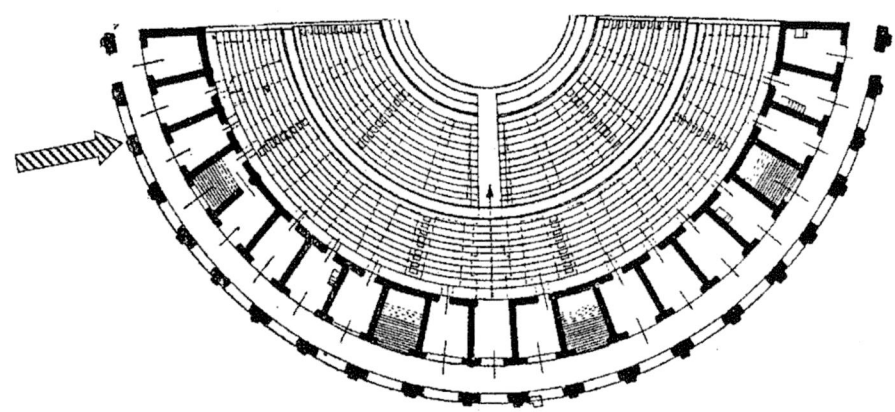

FIGURE 1. PLAN OF THE ROMAN THEATRE OF OSTIA (FROM BUONOPANE 2012: 202) AND TRANSCRIPTIONS OF THE PROBABLE WRITING TESTS (FROM CIL XIV).

---

[3] About the *Officina Lapidaria* and the epigraphic production process see Susini 1966 e 1979; Manacorda 1979; Di Stefano Manzella 1987: 51-57; Donati and Poma (eds) 2012; Tentori Montalto 2014; Carletti 2015.

These quadrangular rooms had a small warehouses in the back, where were found layers of sand and chips residues of marble processing, a large number of sculptural fragments, partially unfinished, and some inscriptions bearing nonsensical sequences of letters (CIL, XIV 5260; 5261; 5256 and 5257), interpretable, probably, as exemples of *probatio scalpri* (Buonopane 2012: 202-203).

The fact that a *marmorarius* produced both inscriptions and generic marble artifacts, and that, then, the craft of stonecutter had no autonomy from that of the sculptor, is also shown in a sign of a workshop in Rome, describing its production of *tituli* and any work in marble.[4] Shop signs (Figure 2) are part of a small group of inscriptions that recall the activity of *scribere titula* such as the famous one from Philippi that lists a series of steps required to engrave an inscription[5] and the signature of the calligrapher *Furius Dionysius Filocalus* on the polished *elogia martyrum* commisioned by pope Damasus in the second half of the 4th century.[6]

CIL VI 9556

CIL VI 9557

CIL X 7296

EDR126742

FIGURE 2. WORKSHOP SIGNS FROM ROME: CIL, VI 9556 (FROM DI STEFANO MANZELLA 1987: 248), 9557 AND EDR126742 (FROM MANACORDA 2000: 290-291) AND PALERMO: CIL, X 7296 (FROM CARLETTI 2015: 358).

---

[4] CIL, VI 9556: '*D(is) M(anibus) / titulos scri/bendos vel / si quid ope/ris marmor/ari opus fu/erit hic ha/bes*'.
[5] It is a sacred inscription that dates back to 2nd -3rd century AD, CIL, III 633.2: '*P(ublius) Hostilius P(ubli) l(ibertus) Philadelphus / petram inferior(em) excidit et titulum fecit ubi / nomina cultor(um) scripsit et sculpsit...* '; CIL, III 633.1: '*P(ublius) Hostilius Philadelphus / ob honor(em) aedilit(atis) titulum polivit / de suo et nomina sodal(ium) inscripsit eorum*'. See Ricci and Nonnis 2007, 49-50, 56.
[6] ED 18 and 27.

Analyzing these epigraphic records it appears clear that there wasn't even a specific technical vocabulary defining the stonecutter himself, the steps and the instruments of the engraving process, but the same generic terms were used for all kinds of stone works. An exception is the verb *ordinare,* that appears in the bilingual shop sign of Palermo.[7] Recently Carlo Carletti (2015: 358-359) proposed to recognize in this hapax a reference to the specific production by the sicilian workshop of monumental inscriptions displayed in public buildings, therefore *ordinare* could mean a preparatory work prior the act of placing the epigraphic object in the preordained space of an architectural structure rather than paginating the text on the stone before the actual letter cutting took place, according to the most common interpretation by Mallon (1955).

Lacking hints from epigraphic evidence and literary sources,[8] it's just the observation of the epigraphs themselves that could help us reconstructing the genesis of an inscription and sometimes even to recognize the peculiarities of a specific workshop. The consistency of some aspects in the layout of the inscriptions - such as type of support, decorations, text organization on writing field - can provide, infact, clues of a common *epigraphic horizon* (Susini 1979).

Referring to the first centuries of the Roman empire carachterized, to say with Panciera (2006: 100), by an unprecedented epigraphic explosion, the huge quantity of inscriptions produced and known nowadays shows us the high level of ability reached by excellent craftsmen, who developed peculiar skills in the making of products easily readable by a large part of the Roman society or at least widely perceptible in figurative and visual terms.

Sculptores became particularly able to choose appropriate supports for each purpose and context, to transfer and arrange the text on the inscribed field and at least to actual carve the graphic forms, cutting the stone with a mallet and a straight edged iron chisel, creating triangular grooves that designe squared block capitals letters, carachterized by a *chiaroscuro* effect and therefore by great clarity (Figure 3).

A series of tricks of the trade - such as the definition of the epigraphic field with frames and moldings, the pagination of the text on the stone's surface with

---

[7] CIL X, 7296: '...*Tituli heic ordinantur et sculpuntur aidibus sacreis qum operum publicorum*'. For an updated analysis of this inscription see Bodel 2014: 747-750.
[8] Generic are the terms used in two of the most cited literary latin source about epigraphy: Petronius (*Satyricon*, 58.7) in the 1st century refers that the libertus Hermeros despite not having studied geometry, arts, rhetoric, however, knew epigraphic writing: '*non didici geometrias, mitica et alogias menias, sed lapidarias litteras scio*'. Sidonius Apollinaris (*Epistolae*, III.12.5) in the 5th century, talking about an inscribed verse epitaph for his grandfather says: '*Quod peto ut tabulae, quantulumcumque est, celeriter indatur; sed vide, ut vitium non faciat in marmore lapidicida; quod factum sive ab industria seu per incuriam mihi magis quam quadratario lividus lector adscribet*'.

FIGURE 3. A STONECUTTER AT WORK (DRAWING: VELIA POLITO).

the symmetrical balance of full and empty spaces, the changes in the module of characters, gaps and margins, the coherent inclusion of decorative elements - were carried out by stonecutters to make their product attractive and to push the reader to focus on the main parts of the text, just like it happens today in graphic design.

Reached the highest point in quality and quantity under Severus, the epigraphic production faced a steep decrease, as showed in Mac Mullen (1982). The deep causes are still debated, but are surely linked with literacy rate, demography and economy. In Late Antiquity, during the so called 'terza età dell'epigrafia' (Donati 1988, 5-6), does this quantitative regression correspond to a qualitative one? Does the natural habit at epigraphic products extremly legible, symmetrical and elegant, endure? And have been those craftsmanships and artistry handed on?

To find an answer to these questions we need again to turn to the epigraphic products themselves, and those from Roman Catacombs, as said before, are a huge and extraordinary consistent sample for the epigraphic habit of this period.

Starting from the choice of the text-bearing object, in the considered inscriptions, we register the frequent use of occasional and reused stone objects, often unsuitable to the purpose (stele, lids and sides of sarcophagus, architectural elements). (Figure 4)

ICVR VII 17585

ICVR I 2813

Figure 4. Reused occasional supports: EDB21639 and EDB32737 (from Epigraphic Database Bari).[*1]

---

* Images and drawings are displayed in EDB records with bibliographic references, when needed, by kind permission of Italian Ministry of Culture (MiBACT) and of the Papal Commission for Sacred Archaeology (PCAS), thanks to a cooperation agreement established with the EAGLE Consortium (CC BY-SA 3.0).

Morever it grows even the reuse of epigraphic materials themeselves with a consequent increase of opistographic tables, employed again even in very short time interval and the outbreak of more disturbing phenomena such as the erasure of the old text to make room for a new one or the introduction of a new text in the interlinear spaces and margins, even inverting the reading direction of the support (Figure 5).

FIGURE 5. MULTIPLE TEXTS ON THE SAME SUPPORT: EDB21490/EDB39651 AND EDB39650 (FROM EPIGRAPHIC DATABASE BARI).

Very significative indicators of a discontinuity with the previous practice are visible in the arrangement of the stone's surface and in the layout of the text. The inscribed field is no longer defined by frames or other expedients. Consequently it can coincide with the whole surface of the support and the text can be arranged asymmetrically or can be completely decentralized. The stone's surface isn't pre-squared with a grid or simple guidance lines, compromising the whole allignement of the text, the justification of the lines and the modular uniformity of letters, as well as the balance in the relationship between text and figurative motifs. It disappears every trick suited to highlighting an internal hierarchy in the text as well as the correspondence of logical and visual units, by breaking words in two or more lines or through the insertion in between of symbols and images. (Figure 6)

Figure 6. Asimmetrical and irregolar disposition of text and images on the inscribed field: EDB34691; EDB21490; EDB33608 and EDB41548 (from Epigraphic Database Bari).

In carving itself the triangular shape incision is increasingly supplanted by the so colled 'a cordone' one, made with a nib pointed chisel, the *subula*, that beaten by the *malleus* perpendicularly to the plane creates traits uneven, heavily chipped or extremely slender, nearly graffiti. (Figure 7)

Figure 7. Examples of 'a cordone' shape incision: EDB18703 and EDB34915 (from Epigraphic Database Bari).

From the standpoint of writing, the block capital become atypical, characterized by a hatch disjointed and modified in the formal structure and, more significatively, by the appearing of elements from new writing systems typically late antique: cursive, minuscule and uncial (Carletti 2012). (Figure 8)

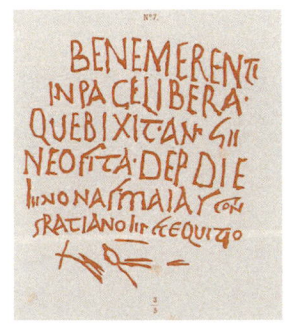
ICVR I 1937

ICVR V 14427

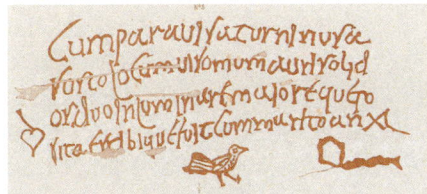
ICVR VII 20669

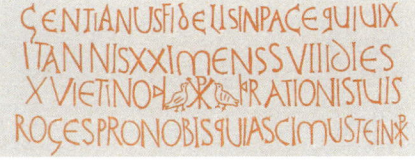
ICVR VIII 22480

FIGURE 8. INSERTION OF CURSIVE, MINUSCULE AND UNCIAL ELEMENT IN CAPITAL BASED INSCRIPTIONS: EDB31855; EDB3384; EDB33627 AND EDB37051 (FROM EPIGRAPHIC DATABASE BARI).

The historical and economic causes of these phenomena could be found in the weakening of the material forms of the city and in the consequent reduction in the quantity and quality of production, that leads to the gradual disappearance of specialized craftsmen and to the need for amateur products when not even for Do It Yourself efforts (Carletti 2015: 365-366).

In the Catacombs we assist at the proliferation of empirical technical procedures, improvised solutions, not supported by proper tools and strongly influenced by the environment in which they are realized, that is frequently the same dark and narrow galleries of underground cemeteries, and by the nature of the supports used or reused, such as inscriptions in mosaic, *opus sectile*, scratched on the walls or on the stones. (Figure 9)

FIGURE 9. THE VARIETY OF EXECUTING TECHNIQUE: EDB22522; EDB15426; EDB24678 AND EDB16094 (FROM EPIGRAPHIC DATABASE BARI).

Among the various techniques that one providing the dipintura of inscriptions in red lead or other colored materials is widespread since the 3rd century in the oldest areas of Roman Catacombs. Supports are made by brickwork elements that close the *loculi*, and in most cases, the paint is applied with a brush, directly on the surface of the support, without any preparation, designing letters in the shape of a lybrarian capital 'rustica' thanks to the flexibility of the instrument. (Figure 10).

A special feature of a few roman funerary contexts is the use of painting inscriptions on layer of mortar and plaster lying, as a preparation, on the bricks elements that close the tomb evidently trying to recreate a marble effect.

The spread of this kind of epitaphs could be explained with the difficult to find stone materials and, moreover, with the cheapness of the product. These inscriptions, as that ones called 'a nastro' (Rocco 2005), traced with a pointed object or even with a finger, on the mortar, still fresh and soft, that seals the *loculus* all around, taking advance of the same elements used for the making of the tomb, require null or minimum expenditure for the support. (Figure 11)

Because they were necessarily made at the same time of the interment of the defunct entrusted to fossores, it is likely that was right on them even the charge of tracing a text, dictated by the relatives of the deceased. It is not inconceivable, however, that in some cases the same family members took care of the material execution of the text, eliminating the separation between composing and inscribing, since the writing is often that one typical of semiliterates, learned during the first years of school.

ICVR IX 25245

ICVR IX 25046

FIGURE 10. PAINTED INSCRIPTIONS ON MARBLE AND BRICKWORK: EDB16027 AND EDB18301 (FROM EPIGRAPHIC DATABASE BARI).

I've tried to summarize the salient features of the epigraphic production from Catacombs, the object of EDB, now we have to analyze how all this deviation from established practice, the beaten track of the title of this meeting, takes effect on encoding and on digital description of the epigraphs.

All epigraphers and encoders are artisans of the digital humanities so we need to analyse the production processes of encoded texts, keeping in mind, just as ancient *lapicidi*, that the final goal is to be extremely clear, using solutions coded and universally avaliable, even if it cannot be underestimated the weight of the personal intervention - if it's true and indeed it is - that editions are interpretations.

EDB consists of a relational database, based on the open-source program MySQL, with a complex scheme drafted according to the most recent advances in epigraphic methodology. The peculiar characterstics of the late antique inscriptions recorded in EDB pose specific issues, not taken into consideration in other similar projects.

ICVR II 6286

Figure 11. Inscription 'a nastro' traced on the mortar: EDB19359
(from Epigraphic Database Bari)

Vocabularies

Considering all the above mentioned and in particular the transformations in the producting process and the spread of different and quite unusual and empirical techniques of execution and of occasional supports, the attributes related to the material nature of the inscription as objects carrying textual information, responding to the questions 'What' and 'How' need to be adapted at classifying the specific and peculiar functions, materials and methods of the inscriptions encoded in EDB, as the traditional epigraphic taxonomies do not totally adhere to their features.

A survey of terminologies intended for description of epigraphic objects in the ICVR volumes has been carried out and has generated lists of controlled terms for the fields *Function, Type of support, Executing technique* (Figure 12). The controlled lists have been integrated in the vocabularies of the EAGLE community[9].

---

[9] http://www.eagle-network.eu/resources/vocabularies/

Type of support	Executing Technicque	Function
Ara	carbone scriptus	Terminus
Architectonica pars	crustis scriptus	Titulus
Arenatum	ex forma	Titulus a viatore scriptus devotionis causa
Cinerarium	exaratus	Titulus acclamatorius
Cippus	insculptus	Titulus apparatus
Instrumentum	non liquet	Titulus dedicatorius
Musivum	pictus	Titulus didascalicus
non liquet	pictus et carbone scriptus	Titulus honorarius
Opus latericium	pictus et insculptus	Titulus sepulchralis
ossum	pictus et scariphatus	Titulus votivus
Sarcophagus	punctim	Add New
Stela	reversus impressione scriptus	
Tabula marmorea	scariphatus	
Tectorium	scariphatus, dein carbone scriptus	
Tectorium induens sepulchrum	signaculo scriptus	
Tofus	tessellis scriptus	
Urna	typo scriptus	
Add New	Add New	

FIGURE 12. CONTROLLED VOCABULARIES FOR TYPE OF SUPPORT, EXECUTING TECHNIQUE AND FUNCTION FIELDS.

Among the features, as you can see in the table above, the list of executing tecniques presents combination of two procedures, a possibility that is unaccounted in other databases, but fits for a small group of EDB records. (Figure 13)

A checkbox allows to annotate if the support is reused or opistographic and more details can be added in the comment box. Considering that every EDB record registers a single epigraphic action, inscriptions written in different moments on the same support can be linked each other associating to bibliographic or online references the value *opistographic* or *reuse*.

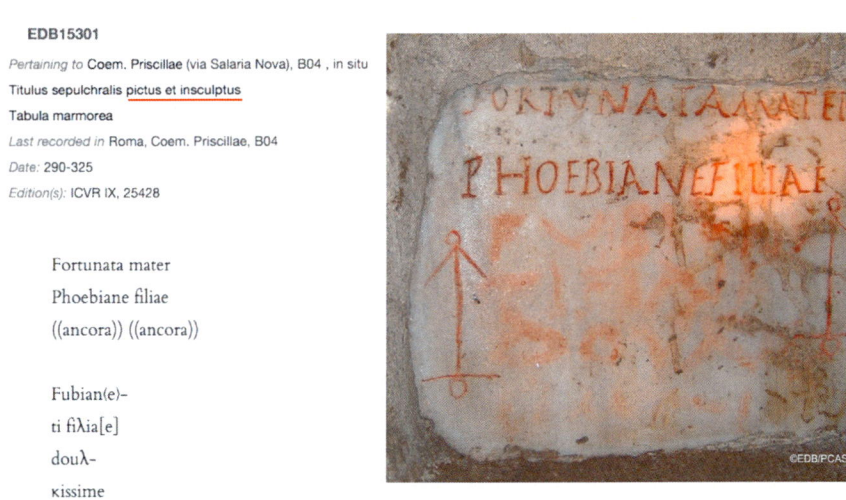

FIGURE 13. ISCRIPTION ENGRAVED AND PAINTED: EDB15301 (FROM EPIGRAPHIC DATABASE BARI).

Multilingual inscriptions

Another specific issue of EDB records is the occurrence of bilingual and/or bigraphic inscriptions, with multiple combination of Greek and Latin alphabets and languages (Figure 14).

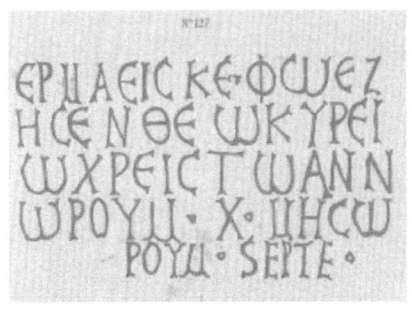
ICVR I 1867

ICVR IX 24315

ICVR VII 18495

Figure 14. Cohexistence of Greek and Latin elements: EDB6231; EDB12309 and EDB13539 (from Epigraphic Database Bari).

The epitaphs, responding to individual needs related to the painful moment of death, could be considered ideal refractive mirror of all these linguistic phenomena, born and developed within the lower social groups. Inscriptions with the coexistence of Greek and Latin elements may reflect directly a language learned in the street or they can be the result of a sophisticated operation or nontheless an error of the writer (Felle 1997: 675). Two checkboxes allow to encode these linguistic combinations: one refers to the presence of Greek Language and Alphabet, the other to the coexistence of Latin and Greek.

'Aberrant' forms

In EDB records we use for the transcriptions the Krummrey - Panciera system (Krummrey and Panciera 1980; Panciera 1991), that has been developed having in mind a standard model of inscription, carefully packaged in a workshop by a skilled artisan. That means that all other 'off the beaten track' epigraphies encounter difficulties in applying it to inscriptions that fall outside this model.

It's the case of the transcription of the so-called 'aberrant' forms, specific and peculiar of the inscriptions of Late Antiquity, when Greek and Latin underwent a gradual transformation and language was enriched with forms of common use.

In EDB, the so-called 'aberrant' forms are not 'normalized' to the 'classical' model, if they are grapho-phonetic outcomes of linguistic modifications of both Latin and Greek, on the contrary, if the compiler recognizes them as outcomes of misstatements and material mistakes of the stonecutter, he transcribes them with the appropriate corrections, following the Krummrey - Panciera conventions. Because in this way a standard query is not able to match with all the inscriptions containing different spellings of a word, to face with this issue each inscription is stored in its original form and in a 'lemmatized' form, where each term is actually replaced with its corresponding lemma, possibly by taking into account its inflexed forms. (Figure 15)

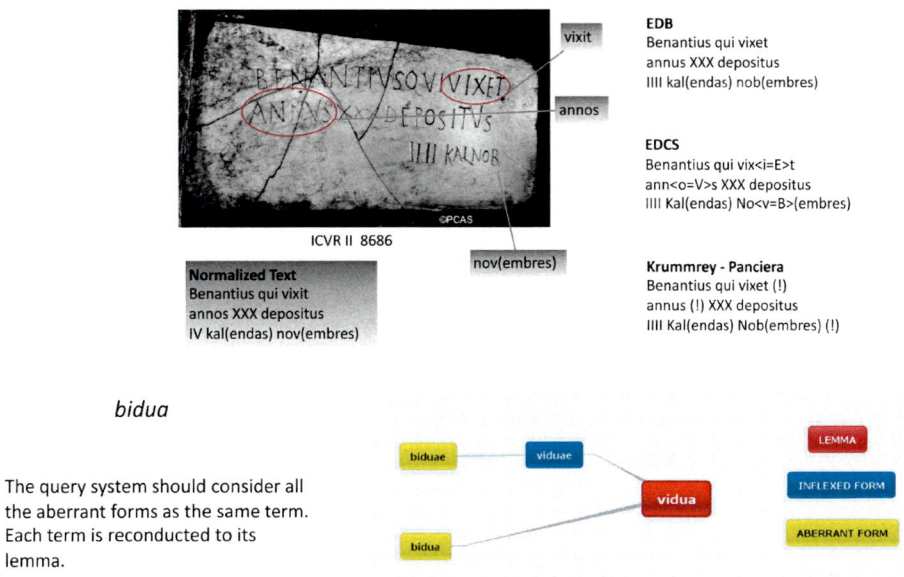

FIGURE 15. DEALING WITH SO-CALLED 'ABERRANT' FORMS
(EDB18067, FROM EPIGRAPHIC DATABASE BARI).

Further developments for this feature concern the possibility of extracting alphabetic lists of words, for exemples the list of all mentioned names and surnames for detailed onomastic studies; the list of all terms, in order to create a *thesaurus*, pursuing the work of Antonio Ferrua (1986) and the list of all the figurative occurencies, with the aim of creating a complex taxonomy of non textual elements, a *thesaurus imaginum* (Felle 2016) inspired by the experience of the *Ancient Graffiti Project* (Benefiel and Sypniewski *supra*).

Direction and orientation of the text

Another significative, and at the moment unresolved issue, is the description of the disposition, the direction and the orientation of the text on the support.

The 'a nastro' inscription showed in figure below has different directions and orientation of writing for each line. In line 2 of the first text the direction is 'up to down' such as in line 3 of the second text, where line 2 is 'clockwise rotated, left to right'.

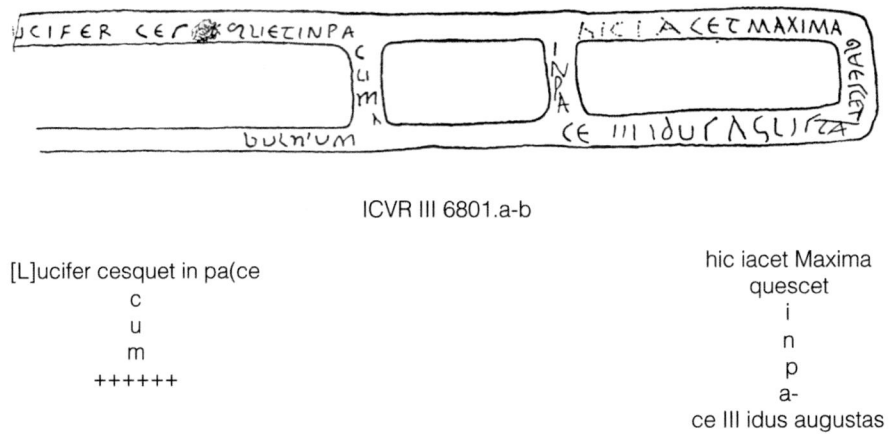

ICVR III 6801.a-b

[L]ucifer cesquet in pa(ce
c
u
m
++++++

hic iacet Maxima
quescet
i
n
p
a-
ce III idus augustas

FIGURE 16. 'A NASTRO' INSCRIPTION (EDB22869/EDB22870) WITH TRANSCRIPTION (FROM EPIGRAPHIC DATABASE BARI).

The Krummrey – Panciera conventions do not provide the possibility to describe the direction and the orientation of the text. In EpiDoc, the XML markup standard for epigraphic documents (Elliot *et al.* 2006-2016), it's possible to add a @rend attribute on the expansion "line-begins" <lb> that precedes each line in an encoded inscription giving a value "left-to-right" or "right-to-left"; other values of @rend can be created in the case of texts written vertically, in a circle or spiral, or otherwise unusually.[10] But these values are not currently handled by the Example Stylesheets, so they cannot be displayed in the transcription.

---

[10] http://www.stoa.org/epidoc/gl/latest/trans-linebreakdirection.html

All these peculiarities are not exclusive for late antique inscriptions from Rome, indeed, they are widely shared with ILA project, infact the solutions proposed by the author and by Giulia Sarullo (*supra*), during the Bari Meeting, could be integrated, and we hope that would be soon adopted by the epigraphic community. For exemple in EDB we decided to use the same arrows symbol as ILA including them into angle brackets precided by colon (Figure 17). The latter brackets in Krummrey Panciera System indicate *litterae omissae quas editorae adiecit* and in EDR have been used, together with colon, for words not written in the text, that the publisher needs to make explicit.

Symbol	Unicode	Direction
〈:↑〉	U+2191	up to down
〈:↓〉	U+2193	down to up
〈:⇁〉	U+2B0E	clockwise rotated left to right
〈:↳〉	U+2B11	counterclockwise rotated left to right
〈:⇀〉	U+2B0F	clockwise rotated right to left
〈:↰〉	U+2B10	counterclockwise rotated right to left

FIGURE 17. UNICODE CHARACTERS REPRESENTING DIRECTIONS AND ORIENTATION OF WRITING.

Using the proposed solutions the text will be displayed in the transcription more clearly and without loss of information (Figure 18).

ICVR III 6801.a-b

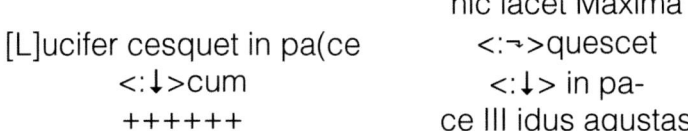

[L]ucifer cesquet in pa(ce
<:↓>cum
++++++

hic iacet Maxima
<:⇁>quescet
<:↓> in pa-
ce III idus agustas

FIGURE 18. TRANSCRIPTIONS OF EDB22869/EDB22870 ACCORDING TO THE SOLUTIONS PROPOSED.

Encoding 'a nastro' inscriptions, remains unresolved the issue of the definition of the dimensions of the support, valid for as well as for the graffiti: do we have to consider the single orizontal and vertical partitions of the mortar between the closing elements or the maximum eight and width of the whole *loculus*?

Text and Images

One more question very urgent for EDB is how to encode the position of the decorative images with respect of the text. The figure below shows a scenario of possibile interactions between verbal and non verbal part of inscriptions.

ICVR II 4469   ICVR VI 15530

ICVR I 2420

FIGURE 19. INTERACTIONS BETWEEN TEXT AND IMAGES: EDB18809, EDB9652 AND EDB32412 (FROM EPIGRAPHIC DATABASE BARI).

A solution that sometimes fits and has been introduced recently in EDB is dividing the text in different parts introducted by a letter precided by a colon inside angle brackets. (Figure 20).

⟨:a⟩

((monogr. Christi in crucem translatum)) ((avis)) ((cantharus)) ((avis))

⟨:b⟩

Μ(α)καριους βιξε

Δεκε(μ)⌈β⌉ρια [---]

⌈β⌉ιξ⌈ε⌉ ανους οκτωτα

b. in tabella ansata; b2. R, lapis; b3. P, O, lapis

FIGURE 20. TRANSCRIPTION OF EDB6444 (ICVR VIII 21163) (FROM EPIGRAPHIC DATABASE BARI).

This solution doesn't fit, however, when we have a non textual element in the middle of a word or a part of the inscription written inside a figurative element (Figure 21).

FIGURE 21. IMAGES IN THE MIDDLE OF THE TEXT: EDB29046; EDB19068; EDB32108 AND TEXT INSIDE THE IMAGE: EDB31546 (FROM EPIGRAPHIC DATABASE BARI).

Even in EpiDoc these features cannot be displayed in the final trascription. It's provided the possibility to insert a section of the text in a separate paragraph <ab> inside a div type="textpart",[11] but this solution refers to divisions of the edited text in fragments or columns and in the stylesheets it generates a marked separation of the parts of the text that would affect its readability.

Concluding, the effort of encoding Christian inscriptions from Rome has made great progress over the last 30 years, enriched by new experiences and projects, particularly thanks to EAGLE Europeana. From the minimalistic version of the 1980s, EDB has been made more accessible and complete, never forgotting the accuracy of the information. Concerning a corpus outside the mainstream epigraphy, EDB has still to face a lot of challenges and unresolved questions, but there is no doubt that the positive atmosphere of cooperation created by EAGLE project, that this meeting exemplifies very clearly, is fostering the exchange of practices and possible solutions, among projects concerning materials far off in time and space, that would probably remained confined in their respective research fields.

---

[11] http://www.stoa.org/epidoc/gl/latest/trans-textpart.html

Bibliography

Bodel, J. 2014. Inscriptions and Literacy. In C. Bruun and J. Edmondson (eds.), *The Oxford Handbook of Roman Epigraphy*: 745-763. Oxford, Oxford University Press.

Buonopane, A. 2012, Un'officina epigrafica e una 'minuta' nel laboratorio di un marmorarius a Ostia? In A. Donati and G. Poma (eds.), *L'officina epigrafica romana: in ricordo di Giancarlo Susini*: 201-206. Faenza, Fratelli Lega.

Carletti, C. 1994. *Inscriptiones christianae urbis Romae, nova series.* Una banca dati. *Vetera Christianorum* 31: 357-368.

Carletti, C. 1997. Introduzione. In A. E. Felle (ed.) *Inscriptiones christianae urbis Romae, tituli graeci. Concordantiae verborum, nominum et imaginum*: vii-xxxiv. Bari, Edipuglia.

Carletti, C. 2012. Minuscole lapidarie. A proposito di un'iscrizione funeraria urbana dell'anno 330. In P. Fioretti (ed.) *Storie di cultura scritta. Studi per Francesco Magistrale*: 223 – 242. Spoleto, Fondazione CISAM.

Carletti, C. 2015. Produzione epigrafica tra Tarda Antichità e Alto Medioevo: discontinuità e tradizione. In A. Molinari, L. Spera and R. Santangeli Valenzani (eds.), *L'archeologia della produzione a Roma (Secoli V-XV). Atti del Convegno Internazionale di Studi (Roma, 27-29 marzo 2014)*: 355-368. Roma, École Française de Rome and Bari, Edipuglia.

Ceci, M., Pio, G. and Rocco, A. 2014. Improving text-based search of inscriptions. In S. Orlandi, R. Santucci, V. Casarosa and P. M. Liuzzo (eds.), *Information Technologies for Epigraphy and Cultural Heritage. Proceedings of the First EAGLE International Conference (Paris, 29-30 September – 1 October 2015)*: 21-30. Roma, Sapienza Università Editrice.

Di Stefano Manzella, I. 1987. *Mestiere di epigrafista. Guida alla schedatura del materiale epigrafico lapideo.* Roma, Quasar.

Donati A. and Poma G. (eds.) 2012, *L'officina epigrafica romana: in ricordo di Giancarlo Susini*. Faenza, Fratelli Lega.

ED. A. Ferrua (ed.) *Epigrammata damasiana,* 1942. Città del Vaticano, Pontificio Istituto di Archeologia Cristiana.

EG. M. Guarducci (ed.), *Epigrafica Greca*. I-IV, 1967-78. Roma, Istituto Poligrafico dello Stato.

Elliott, T., Bodard, G. and Cayless, H. *et al.* 2006-2016. Epigraphic Documents in TEI XML. Online material: http://epidoc.sf.net.

Elliott, T., Bodard, G., Mylonas, E., Stoyanova, S., Tupman, C., Vanderbilt, S. *et al.* (2007-2014). EpiDoc Guidelines: Ancient documents in TEI XML. Version 8.21. http://www.stoa.org/epidoc/gl/latest/

Felle A. E. (ed.) 1997. *Inscriptiones christianae urbis Romae, tituli graeci. Concordantiae verborum, nominum et imaginum.* Bari, Edipuglia.

Felle, A. E. 2007. Fenomeni di compresenza delle lingue e delle scritture greca e latina nella epigrafia romana di committenza cristiana. In M. Mayer i Olivé, G. Baratta and Al. Guzmán Almagro (eds.), *Acta XII Congressus Internationalis Epigraphiae Graecae et Latinae. Provinciae Imperii Romani inscriptionibus descriptae (Barcelona, 3-8 septembris 2002)*: 475-481, Barcelona, Institut d'estudis catalans.

Felle, A. E. 2012. Esperienze diverse e complementari nel trattamento digitale delle fonti epigrafiche: il caso di EAGLE ed EpiDoc. In N. Palazzolo (ed.), *Diritto romano e scienze antichistiche nell'era digitale. Convegno di studio (Firenze, 12-13 settembre 2011), Collectanea Graeco-Romana. Studi e strumenti per la ricerca storico-giuridica*, 10: 117-130. Torino, Giappichelli.

Felle, A. E. 2014. Perspectives on the digital corpus of the Christian inscriptions of Rome (Epigraphic Database Bari). Contexts and texts. *Zeitschrift für Papyrologie und Epigraphik* 191: 302-307.

Felle, A. E. and Zimmermann, N. 2014. A Case of Interaction between Research Projects: The Epigraphic Database Bari and the Domitilla Projekt. In S. Orlandi, R. Santucci, V. Casarosa and P. M. Liuzzo (eds.), *Information Technologies for Epigraphy and Cultural Heritage. Proceedings of the First EAGLE International Conference*: 75-96. Roma, Sapienza Università Editrice.

Felle, A. E. 2016. Visual features of Inscriptions. An issue for EDB (and EAGLE). In S. Orlandi, R. Santucci, F. Mambrini and P. M. Liuzzo (eds.), *Digital and Traditional Epigraphy in Context. Proceedings of the Second EAGLE International Conference (Rome, 27-29 January 2016)*: 91-106. Roma, Sapienza Università Editrice.

Ferrua, A. 1986. *Note al Thesaurus Linguae Latinae: addenda et corrigenda (A-D)*. Bari, Edipuglia.

IC. *Inscriptiones christianae urbis Romae septimo saeculo antiquiores*, I-II, I.B. de Rossi (ed.), I-II, 1857-1861; *Supplementum*, G. Gatti (ed.) 1915. Romae, ex officina libraria pontificia.

ICVR. *Inscriptiones christianae urbis Romae septimo saeculo antiquiores. Nova series*. I-X, 1922-1992. A. Silvagni, A. Ferrua, D. Mazzoleni, C. Carletti (eds), Romae, ex officina libraria doct. Befani and Civitate Vaticana, Pontificium Institutum Archaeologiae Christianae.

Krummrey, H. and Panciera, S. 1980. Criteri di edizione e segni diacritici. *Tituli* 2: 205-215.

Mallon, J. 1955. L'*ordinatio* des inscriptions. *Comptes rendus de l'Académie des Inscriptions et Belles-Lettres* 99: 126-137.

Mac Mullen, R. 1982, The Epigraphic Habit in the Roman Empire. *American Journal of Philology* 103: 233-246.

Manacorda, D. 1979, *Un'officina lapidaria sulla via Appia: studio archeologico sull'epigrafia sepolcrale d'età giulio-claudia in Roma*. Roma, L'Erma di Bretschneider.

Manacorda, D. 2000. Archeologia e epigrafia: problemi di metodo a proposito di CIL VI 8960. In A. Buko and P. Urbańczyk (eds.), *Archeologia w teorii i w praktyce*: 277-293. Warszawa, Instytut Archeologii i Etnologii Polskiej Akademii Nauk.

Panciera, S. 1991. Struttura dei Supplementi e segni diacritici: dieci anni dopo. *Supplementa Italica* n.s. 8: 9-21.

Panciera, S. 2006. L'epigrafia latina nel passaggio dalla Repubblica all'Impero. In S. Panciera, *Epigrafi, epigrafia, epigrafisti. Scritti vari editi e inediti (1956-2005) con note complementari e indici*: 83-101. Roma, Quasar.

Panciera, S., Eck, W., Manacorda, D. and Tedeschi, C. 2006. Questioni di metodo. Il monumento iscritto come punto d'incontro tra epigrafia, archeologia, paleografia e storia (a proposito dei primi tre volumi di Supplementa Italica – Imagines). *Scienze dell'Antichità* 13: 583-660.

Ricci, C. and Nonnis, D. 2007. Scriptura e scriptores: alcune riflessioni sul mondo romano. In G. Fiorentino (eds), *Scrittura e Società. Storia, Cultura, Professioni*: 33-56. Roma, Aracne.

Rocco, A. 2005. Le iscrizioni 'a nastro' nel cimitero di Commodilla a Roma. *Atti della Pontificia Accademia Romana di Archeologia. Memorie*, III serie in 8°, VI: 263-445, Roma, Quasar.

Rocco, A. 2015. Risorse digitali per la ricerca storica: l'esempio di EDB, database delle iscrizioni dei cristiani di Roma. In A. Giudice and G. Rinaldi (eds.), *Realia Christianorum. Il contributo delle fonti documentarie allo studio del cristianesimo antico. Atti del Convegno (Napoli, 14 novembre 2014)*: 189-208. Bologna, Ante Quem.

Rocco, A. 2016. EDB 2.0. How Eagle Europeana Project improved the Epigraphic Database Bari. In S. Orlandi, R. Santucci, F. Mambrini and P. M. Liuzzo (eds.), *Digital and Traditional Epigraphy in Context. Proceedings of the Second EAGLE International Conference (Rome, 27-29 January 2016)*: 73-90. Roma, Sapienza Università Editrice.

Susini, G. 1966. *Il lapicida romano*. Bologna, Arti grafiche Tamari.

Susini, G. 1979. Officine epigrafiche: problema di storia del lavoro e della cultura. In *Actes du VIIe Congrès international d'épigraphie grecque et latine (Costantza, 9-15 septembre 1977)*: 45-62. Bucuresti-Paris, Editura Academiei.

Tentori Montalto, M. 2014. Il lapicida greco. *Epigraphica* 76: 17-46.

Challenges of Byzantine Epigraphy in the 21st Century. A Short Note[1]

Andreas Rhoby
Austrian Academy of Sciences, Institute for Byzantine Studies - Vienna

Before presenting a general overview about current challenges in the field of Byzantine epigraphy, I would like to say a few words about the current state of research in this field and I would also like to comment on the definition of the term. In 1991, Cyril Mango, one of the few leading experts in late antique and Byzantine epigraphy, stated that 'A discipline of Byzantine epigraphy does not yet exist.' (Mango 1991). This criticism does not mean that there had been no endeavors to promote the proper analysis of early Christian Greek and Byzantine inscriptions. On the contrary, the creation of a corpus of Byzantine inscriptions has been considered an urgent need since the nineteenth century when first systematic collections were compiled, such as the *Corpus Inscriptionum Graecarum* series, which was published at the Prussian Academy of Sciences in Berlin (For detailed analysis consult Rhoby 2015).

Unfortunately, the situation has not changed much since Mango's statement because no handbook on or detailed introduction to Byzantine epigraphy with a specific focus on middle and late Byzantine inscriptions (700–1500 AD) has been published to date. However, especially in the last few years, Byzantine epigraphy and the discussions about its importance and relevance for other research fields have again received attention. When - within the framework of the Association Internationale des Études Byzantines (AIEB) and its epigraphy commission[2] - the idea of a new publication series for Byzantine inscriptions came up, we had to define what the term 'Byzantine epigraphy' stands for:[3] does it encompass all inscriptions which were produced on Byzantine territories between the fourth and the fifteenth centuries? This would mean that not only Greek but also Latin, Arabic, Slavonic, Armenian, Georgian, and inscriptions in other languages should be considered. But how should one deal with medieval Greek inscriptions which were produced outside the Byzantine Empire such as in the Near East after the Arab conquest, in Southern Italy up to the fourteenth century, long after the end of the Byzantine rule, or on the Northern coast of the Black Sea? How should

---

[1] This short note is an updated and slightly enlarged version (including footnotes) of the oral presentation, which was given at the meeting 'Off the Beaten Track. Epigraphy at the Borders' (Sixth EAGLE International Event, Bari, September 24-25, 2015).
[2] http://www.aiebnet.gr/en/commissions.html. The commission, based in Vienna, is chaired by Peter Schreiner and coordinated by me.
[3] Cf. Mango 2011: 59; Mango 2015: 33-35.

one proceed with 'Protobulgarian' inscriptions[4] for which the Greek language and script were used? There is a lot of *pro* and *contra* to be considered in the discussion of these vital questions.

Before - again within the framework of AIEB's epigraphy commission - the new publication series *Inscriptiones Graecae Aevi Byzantini* (IGAB) was launched, it was decided, for reasons of feasibility, to focus (as the title suggests) on Greek inscriptions. As of 2016, no volume of this IGAB series has been published, but several volumes are in progress, such as the edition of the Greek inscriptions of Crete between the thirteenth and seventeenth centuries supervised by Vasiliki Tsamakda.[5]

It must be stressed that IGAB does not make any claims regarding being a 'corpus.' The motivation behind its creation was the desire to have a publication format in which Byzantine Greek inscriptions (regardless of their origin, their time limit, their genre and so forth) could be published according to fixed editorial guidelines which are based on the French series of medieval Latin inscriptions, 'Corpus des inscription de la France médiévale.'[6] The template looks as follows:

Title (+ date)

A) function

B) place (either *in situ* or in museum, collection etc.; mention of autopsy)

C) material, measures

D) transcription (ideally with Athena Ruby font)[7]

D1) transliteration

[D2) in exceptional cases 'literary' edition]

E) translation (either into English, French, German or Italian)

F) earlier editions and literature

G) paleographic analysis

---

[4] Beševliev 1992.
[5] http://web.rgzm.de/forschung/schwerpunkte-und-projekte/a/article/die-griechischen-inschriften-kretas-13-17-jh.html.
[6] http://cescm.labo.univ-poitiers.fr/poles-editoriaux/corpus-des-inscriptions-de-la-france-medievale/.
[7] Cf. infra, p. 89.

H) linguistic analysis

I) commentary on political, cultural and art history etc.

J) image

[some categories may be omitted!]

The IGAB edition platform is, of course, open to both paper and online publications which meet the expectations of twenty-first century research standards.

There is common agreement on the fact that technological advances have already opened up new possibilities for displaying inscriptions.

A tool of considerable value for early Greek Christian and Byzantine inscriptions is the 'Searchable Greek Inscriptions Database' of the Packard Humanities Institute, first published as a CD-ROM and now available online.[8] A more elaborate digital edition of early Christian and Byzantine inscriptions was created by Charlotte Roueché, who turned her book about the Late Roman and Byzantine inscriptions of Aphrodisias[9] into a database.[10] There is a consensus that this database can serve as a model for future digital editions of Byzantine inscriptions (Roueché 2009; Roueché 2015), and there are more databases which have been completed since then, including the digital editions of the inscriptions of Roman Tripolitania,[11] as well as the online corpus 'Ancient Inscriptions of the Northern Black Sea.'

These digital editions are based on EpiDoc, which is 'an international, collaborative effort that provides guidelines and tools for encoding scholarly and educational editions of ancient documents' using 'a subset of the Text Encoding Initiative's (TEI) standard for the representation of texts in digital form using the Extensible Markup Language (XML).'[12]

The recently launched online corpus 'Ancient Inscriptions of the Northern Black Sea, vol. V: Byzantine inscriptions'[13] is indeed a very valuable tool for several reasons: first, because it offers the entire Greek inscriptional material from a remote area of Byzantine influence, which was previously only accessible in

---

[8] Greek Documentary Texts. (1) Inscriptions, (2) Papyri. CD-ROM 7. The Packard Humanities Institute, 1991–1996, http://epigraphy.packhum.org/inscriptions/. The Epigraphische Datenbank Heidelberg database covers Latin inscriptions (http://edh-www. adw.uni-heidelberg.de/home?lang=de) as does the Epigraphic Database Bari (http://www.edb.uniba.it/), which also includes Greek inscriptions.
[9] Roueché 1989.
[10] http://insaph.kcl.ac.uk/ala2004/. New version with inscriptions found up to the end of 1994 http://insaph.kcl.ac.uk/index.html.
[11] http://inslib.kcl.ac.uk/irt2009/.
[12] http://www.stoa.org/epidoc/gl/latest/; http://sourceforge.net/p/epidoc/wiki/Home/. All the EpiDoc projects are listed at http://www.stoa.org/epidoc/gl/latest/app-bibliography.html
[13] http://iospe.kcl.ac.uk/index.html.

rare and mostly outdated publications. Secondly, because by making use of the EpiDoc system it allows various search options, for example, for 'Origin of Text', 'Category of Text', or 'Dating Criteria.'

As useful as the database is, one must not forget that it took an enormous effort to create it. A lot of researchers were involved,[14] especially technicians for the programming work and the conversion of the data into XML format. One of the future challenges of similar endeavors will, therefore, be successful applications for funding. Further challenges include the question of sustainability: with regard to the inscriptions in the Northern Black Sea database, many of them were published there for the first time; others were edited in publications which are very difficult to access.[15]

Particularly in the case of Byzantine epigraphy, we still have to use editions which date back to the nineteenth century or are at least one hundred years old. Is there any guarantee that the Northern Black Sea database will still be accessible thirty years from now? In my view - with regard to Byzantine inscriptions for which reliable editions are very sparse - the ideal approach to the question of the most useful way to publish them is to go both ways: despite the fact that the number of inscriptions which were produced in the middle and late Byzantine period is bigger than one might expect, it is still much more manageable than the number of ancient inscriptions. This means that we are dealing with smaller corpora which can be edited in paper publications that can then be transformed into digital publications - such as in the EpiDoc format - making use of manifold search and display options. Such a corpus with a manageable number of inscriptions is the recently completed three-volume edition of Byzantine metrical inscriptions dating between 600 and 1500 (Rhoby 2009-2014): it comprises ca. 800 epigrams which are preserved on stone, frescoes, mosaics, portable object, icons etc. It is my aim - and it was also the urgent demand of a recent review (Lauxtermann 2014) - to produce a multidimensional database from this material.

Another issue I would like to raise is the presentation of the specific graphic shapes of Greek letters used in Byzantine inscriptions and forms and variations which characterize Byzantine texts. The differentiation of letters is an important way of classifying chronologically those inscriptions to which no date is appended. In former publications, both on paper and online, no specific attention was paid to reproducing letter forms, either because no font set was available or because the edition was accompanied by an image in which the script could be recognized.

---

[14] http://iospe.kcl.ac.uk/project/team.html.
[15] E.g. the publications by VV. Latyshev: see http://iospe.kcl.ac.uk/inscriptions/bibliography.html.

The launch of the new Athena Ruby font created at Dumbarton Oaks generates more possibilities for the *grosso modo* accurate representation of (Byzantine) inscriptions, not only for those preserved on coins and seals.[16] It is an OpenType, Unicode-compliant font, and therefore compatible with all major operating systems. Originally created for the proper display of Greek letters, their combinations, ligatures and abbreviations used on Byzantine lead seals, this font can also be used for the visual transcription of inscriptions on other media. For the aforementioned corpus of Greek inscriptions from the island of Crete, it was decided to use the font for the first transcription (no. D) according to the IGAB template. The discussion among scholars of Byzantine epigraphy as to whether applying the Athena Ruby font is a convenient application for further future editions remains open.

In conclusion: the main duty for the discipline of Byzantine epigraphy for the future is to create proper editions - regardless of whether on paper or digital - with translations and commentaries. A further challenge will be to draw the academic community's attention to the importance of the Byzantine inscriptional heritage. For decades the significance of inscriptions as a source for Byzantine civilization had been considered rather small. However, the amount of the preserved material - as stated, ca. 800 metrical inscriptions, not counting the epigrams which are transmitted in manuscripts only - should enable us to appreciate them as a valuable testimony.

Proper training for scholars interested in Byzantine epigraphy is also needed: the study of Byzantine inscriptions should, therefore, be part of university *curricula* for Byzantine Studies as are other 'auxiliary' disciplines;[17] moreover, special summer schools, both for established scholars and students, with hands-on-sessions in museums and excursions to attractive sites should be offered, as was, for example, the case for a master class in Byzantine epigraphy organized by Ida Toth and me at the British School of Archaeology in Athens in 2014[18] which will be repeated on a biennial or triennial basis.

---

[16] http://www.doaks.org/resources/athena-ruby; see Kalvesmaki 2015.
[17] An exception is Oxford University, where classes on Byzantine epigraphy are offered regularly by Ida Toth: http://www.history.ox.ac.uk/faculty/staff/profile/toth/research.html.
[18] http://www.oeaw.ac.at/byzanz/pdf/summer_workshop_byzantine_epigraphy.pdf.

Bibliography

Beševliev, V. 1992. *Părvo-bălgarski nadpisi (2., preraboteno i dop. izd.)*. Sofia, Izdat. na Balgarskata Akad. na Naukite.

Kalvesmaki, J. 2015. Introducing Athen Ruby, Dumbarton Oaks' New Font for Byzantine Inscriptions. In Rhoby 2015: 121-126.

Lauxtermann, M. 2014. *Anzeiger für die Altertumswissenschaft* 67: 207-211.

Mango, C. 1991. Epigraphy. In *Oxford Dictionary of Byzantium*: 711-713. New York -Oxford, Oxford University Press.

Mango, C. 2011. What is a Byzantine Inscription? In *Proceedings of the 22nd International Congress of Byzantine Studies, Sofia, 22-27 August 2011*: II, 59. Sofia, Bulgarian Historical Heritage Foundation.

Mango, C. 2015. Some Lessons of Byzantine Epigraphy. In Rhoby 2015: 33-35.

Rhoby, A. 2009-2014. *Byzantinische Epigramme in inschriftlicher Überlieferung*. Vienna, Verlag der Österreichischen Akademie der Wissenschaften.

Rhoby, A. (ed.) 2015, *Inscriptions in Byzantium and Beyond. Methods – Projects – Case Studies*. Vienna, Verlag der Österreichischen Akademie der Wissenschaften.

Rhoby, A. 2015a. A Short History of Byzantine Epigraphy. In Rhoby 2015: 17-29.

Roueché, Ch. 1989. *Aphrodisias in Late Antiquity. The Late Roman and Byzantine Inscriptions. With contributions by J.M. Reynolds*. London, Society for the Promotion of Roman Studies.

Roueché, Ch. 2009. Digitizing inscribed text. In: M. Deegan and K. Sutherland (eds.), *Text Editing, Print and the Digital World:* 159-168. Farnham, Ashgate.

Roueché, Ch. 2015. Byzantine Epigraphy for the 21st Century. In Rhoby 2015: 115- 119.

EDV
Italian Medieval Epigraphy in the Vernacular (9th-15th century). A new Database

Luna Cacchioli - Nadia Cannata - Alessandra Tiburzi
Epigraphic Database of documents in the Vernacular -
'Sapienza' University of Rome[1]

Introduction

EDV aims at providing scholars, students and the general public with a flexible and user-friendly database cataloguing all inscriptions *in volgare* (as we commonly define them in Italian, i.e. written in modern languages deriving from Latin), which were produced in Italy during the centuries spanning from the 9th to the 15th. The project includes inscriptions executed on whatever surface (stone, plaster, canvas, cloth, glass, terracotta, iron and other metals etc.) and intended for some form of public exposure.

The inscriptions thus identified may have served a wide variety of different functions, which we have loosely classified into the following four categories:

1. **Public notices** (texts with an identifiable public purpose carrying a message of public interest addressed to a given social group).
   These may be further classified as:
   (a) *normative inscriptions* (edicts, laws, etc.);
   (b) *funerary inscriptions* (tombstones and other forms of remembrance);
   (c) *commemorative inscriptions* (memories of events, ex-voto etc.);
   (d) *dedicatory inscriptions* (made as some form of acknowledgment for patronage).
2. **Captions and explanatory notes** such as artists's signatures, or explanatory captions in paintings; messages of a didascalic or moralizing nature (proverbs, adages etc.).
3. **Graffiti and other casual and extemporaneous writings**. These date from the very early examples of the annotations on the *formelle of the Cattedra di San Pietro* (9th century AD) to the 13th century AD (Tarquinia

---

[1] This article was written in cooperation by the three authors. Nadia Cannata is responsible for the first three paragraphs ('Introduction'; 'The nature of the database'; 'Oral voices and literary languages: some considerations'), Alessandra Tiburzi wrote the following 'Classifying the materials' and, in the last one, 'Other issues and some proposed solutions'; Luna Cacchioli the other subparagraphs: 'Linguistic Variety'; 'How to publish inscriptions featuring in complex iconographic constructions'. All the photos are by the authors: to the best of their knowledge the photographed monuments are not subject to copyright limitations.

Tomba Bartoccini), or the graffiti from Foligno at the *Casa dei pittori Mazzaforte* (1468-76).
4. **Inscriptions on objects of everyday use**.

We count, as of today, around 440 extant inscriptions and about a dozen presumably destroyed, but known through secondary sources. The numbers are constantly rising, particularly as we come by information on inscriptions produced in the South of Italy and other areas for which documentation is scant. The best studied areas are, perhaps not surprisingly, Central Italy, Rome, Tuscany and the Veneto. The distribution of the material can be seen in the following graph:

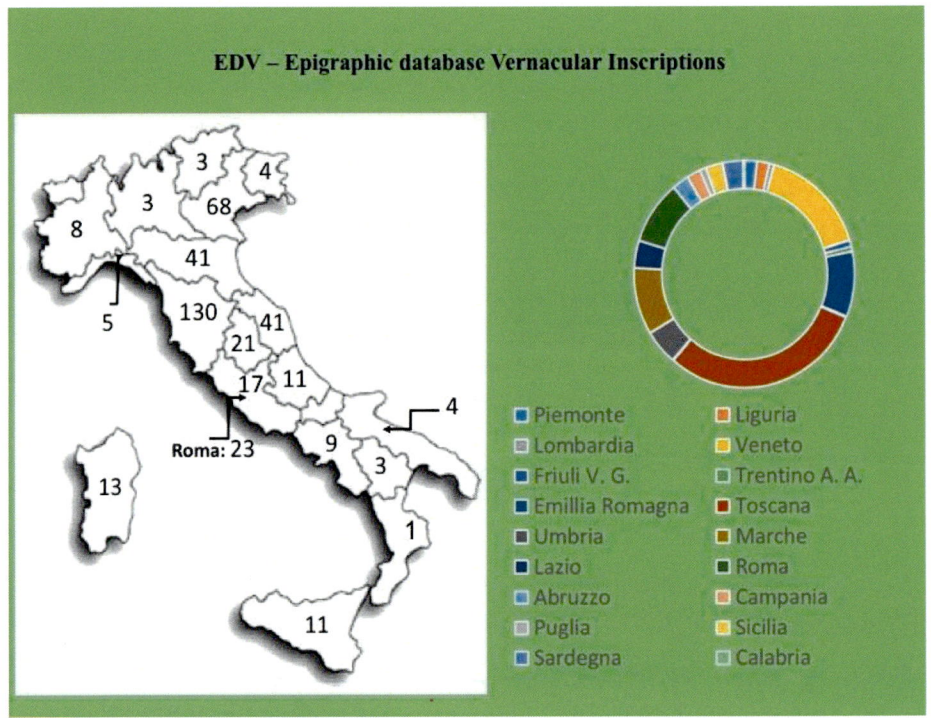

Figure 1. The distribution of the material.

The material so far collected is characterized, first and foremost, by its extraordinary variety in terms of form and function as well as language and style. We have inscriptions in French from Piedmont, Umbria, Campania, Veneto; inscriptions in Catalan and Sardinian, and in the whole array of different *volgari* in use in Italy in the early modern period. Some of them have not enjoyed a written tradition rich enough to afford them with a name, so they are defined by their geographical area only (see Appendix).

There are vernacular inscriptions written in Greek alphabet from Apulia (Soleto, Lecce, Chiesa di Santo Stefano, *Didascalie del giudizio universale*, 1347) but also when – as in the vast majority of cases – Latin alphabet is used, its graphemes may acquire, according to time and space, very different and at times not unequivocal meanings. Some inscriptions are in verses, some quote pieces of literature or echo psalms or some other biblical text, and some are just plainly informative or even shabbily composed. As for forms, materials and surfaces we have inscriptions carved, painted or written on stone, plaster, canvass, iron, terracotta, ceramics, gold, silver, bronze, ivory, mosaics, cloth, glass, wood.

The nature of the database

Why are they part of a single database then? Curiously enough their definition as a unit is warranted by the variety of languages they use, or rather by the Latin they do not use. Such a definition by subtraction (or by absence) for the time and place considered does indeed amount to a unifying feature. We know that Dante, together with his contemporaries, considered that Latin, known only to a minority of learned people, was provided *naturaliter* with a solid, homogeneous and unique written tradition because of its being an artificial language. All other contemporary languages, on the other hand, shared the common feature of being natural, and as such familiar to all sectors of society, but limited to everyday use and mostly oral. This in turn explained for him their variety – perceived even in terms of inexplicable volatility and even arbitrariness – and their differences in space, time and even within the very same nation, as well as their lack of a written form, let alone tradition.

It was Dante's contention that such a tradition may, and indeed should be acquired, but also that the process to be initiated was complex and that imposing onto the vernacular a unified linguistic canon in terms of language and style would happen in defiance of its very nature. Those who wrote public and private inscriptions in their native languages shared that contention, naturally, and it so happened that some of the users of vernaculars, however *sanza lettere*, measured themselves with the challenge. They constitute a homogeneous group in terms of Italian cultural history and deserve to be considered in context as trying to break the constraints of the *diglossia* in which medieval Europe and Italy more than other regions appeared to be locked.

Oral voices and literary languages. A few considerations

It may be perceived as a truism that a written document, being a document of writing, is also a document of written culture and of the culture of writing. That is to say that it must testify to the processes which have enabled a linguistic culture to became also a written culture. If one analyses in greater depth the implications of such apparent puns their seeming banality may give way to a more problematic dimension and convey issues which are more complex than usually meets the eye.

The process of translating language into script is by no means a mechanical one, and every society has dealt with it differently: adopting scripts, alphabets, entrusting certain sectors of society with the responsibility of writing and preserving memory of a tradition, and eventually by electing one linguistic variety as the best suited for the task. Latin enjoyed that role for a millennium, but around the period we are focusing on that primacy was being put into question, due to the lamentable fact that it was no longer widely understood. The void this left can be easily seen if one considers the array of different Romance varieties which were, for better or worse, put into writing, in a collective effort of electing one variety which might serve the purpose, which was shared across the peninsula – despite its division.

The materials we are studying are a living testimony to the intricacies of this process and as such constitute a homogeneous group which deserves to be studied as a unit. The hope is that it may return further insight on the history of the Italian vernaculars which is a fundamental component of the history of Italian as a great European language of culture: such history can in no way be abstracted or severed from the history of the ways through which vernaculars acquired a written form, which form they acquired, and why. No vernacular graduated to becoming a language without the endowment of a written tradition. Why did some vernaculars acquire it and others did not?

Writing is not necessarily, although all too often we consider and use it as if it were, a document of the way people spoke in the time and place of production of a particular document. This is so not only because standardized language – as any written language is by means of its function – is not native to anyone (Johnson 1987) but more importantly because the act of writing presupposes a cultural mediation which is in itself a historical document, begging to be described, interpreted and understood. Writing only documents the ways in which a group which perceives itself as such chose to solve the problem of transposing language into a transferable and repeatable form. Writing is not co-substantial to humanity, or at least not in the way speaking is. The act of translating speech into a symbolic dimension, mostly – but not exclusively – for the sake of memory and preservation is not an act that has been performed in all known human societies, nor – when indeed it was performed – one may count on any consistency in the ways that such a complex operation was carried out. It is our firm conviction that any written document in order to 'speak' needs to be approached as a testimony of how, when, why and thanks to whom a message acquired a written form, well before it may be discussed in its linguistic, ethnographic, anthropological or indeed any other significance.

This project started off as a study of the uses of the vernacular in Italy in public lettering and namely as a pilot scheme to investigate an area of linguistic usage which has been little explored: uses of mother tongues, as opposed to Latin, in public epigraphic contexts, as part of an enquiry into the use of languages other than Latin in Medieval Italy and what do they contribute to our knowledge of the linguistic culture of the time.

In fact the data, if anything, testify to a geography and history of linguistic usage in Italy that defuses any conception which may still be left of a linear and inexorable development of the language from shack and multiple beginnings to a solid universal and single standard. History went rather more in circles, with borrowings and innovations alternating constantly. There are inscriptions in Tuscan produced in Sardinia, inscriptions in Tuscan designed and produced in Tuscany for the Duomo in Monreale by Bonanno Pisano in the 12th century, and – conversely – also a blanket in Sicilian produced for the Tuscan Guicciardini family in the 15th century, and this is to name but a few.

In our research we have joined forces with the Dipartimento di Scienze dell'Antichità at Sapienza University of Rome, where Silvia Orlandi, Gianluca Gregori and Maria Letizia Caldelli have been nourishing an outstanding tradition in Roman Epigraphy, with the flexibility to look beyond the Classical Period. In our Faculty there is also a very strong tradition in Medieval Studies and more to the point in Palaeography, History of Writing and Medieval Epigraphy. All were generous enough to embrace our endeavours and therefore we have the privilege to be able to discuss issues relating to the construction of our database, the digitization of the materials and the structure of our projected *EDV – Epigraphic Database of documents in the Vernacular* with colleagues specializing in other fields which gives us the opportunity of taking advantage of expertise on language, history of writing and history of written records.

Classifying the materials

Our corpus, as defined above, is a rather complex object to classify with any scientific coherence, due its extraordinary variety in terms of language, functions, use, materials and also the sheer extension of the territory of its production (the Italian peninsula) and the wide time span considered (9th-15th century).

Robert Favreau (1997: 5) in his *Épigraphie médiévale* claimed that to define epigraphy, 'il faut (…) partir non de la forme, mais des fonctions de l'inscription'. Moving from that assumption we have devised a classification of the material based first of all on the function intended for the script, which determined the choice of language, surface, and to an extent even script. It is a well known fact in the history of written culture that where and how one writes depends mostly on why one writes and, of course, also on who is writing.

In order to devise our main functional categories the studies of Francesco Sabatini (1996 and 1997), Livio Petrucci (2010) and the *Corpus Inscriptiones Medii Aevi*

Italiae (Cimarra *et al.* 2002) have guided our reasoning. Francesco Sabatini introduced a functional classification which distinguished: 'iscrizioni in funzione di un testo figurativo'; 'iscrizioni in simbiosi con un testo figurativo' and 'iscrizioni autonome' (Sabatini 1996: 569-576; 1997: 177-183); Livio Petrucci (2010: 41-68), on his part, adopted six different classes for the description of his material: captions, epitaphs, signatures, moral admonitions, civic memories, piety. The *Corpus Inscriptiones Medii Aevi Italiae* distinguishes between: '[iscrizioni] funerarie, commemorative – dedicatorie, celebrative – onorifiche, esortative – propiziatorie – augurali, didascaliche – esegetiche, diplomatiche, segnaletiche, *tabulae lusorie*, sigle, monogrammi, firme, iscrizioni estemporanee' (Cimarra *et al.* 2002: VII).

On our part we have decided to classify the material in three macro-categories, as already detailed: public notices; captions and explanatory notes; extemporaneous materials; writings on objects of everyday use.

All categories are further divided into sub-categories, which we shall now discuss in greater detail.

Public notices

These include all inscriptions produced with for a civic function (Petrucci 1997: 57). They were intended for a public exposure and their author is always identifiable (Sabatini 1997: 182-183).

Normative inscriptions

These include all public notices publishing chapters, laws, *chartae lapidariae* and in general information of relevance to the whole community. In this category we find e.g. the so-called *Lastra della carta bambagina* (14th century), visible in the Museo Civico Medievale in Bologna. It hung in the Palazzo Pubblico and ruled on the measurements of paper which was to be produced in Bologna: *Queste sieno le forme del chomune di Bollo/gna de che grandeça dene essere le charte de ba(m)/baxe che se farano in Bollogna esso destreto ch/ome qui de sotto e divixado:/ inperialle/ realle/ meçane / reçute* (Breveglieri 1997: 86).

To the same category belongs the *Iscrizione dei fanciulli della Pietà* from Venice (14th century, first half) walled in Campo Sant'Angelo, which was probably written in the vernacular to maximise the audience of potential benefactors of the Ospedale della Pietà. It offered *indulgenze* in exchange for charity: + *Papa Climento sexsto di uno / anno xl dì de perdon, çaschuno / che porce lemusena ali fantoli/ni dela Pie/tade. Miser lo patriarcha / de Grado, miser lo vescodo de / Castelo xl dì. / Suma lo p(er)do dela pia/tade uno anno cxx dì / ed a(l)tre gracie molte* (Stussi 1997: 164).

FIGURE 2. VENICE, CAMPO SANT'ANGELO, INSCRIPTION OF FANCIULLI DELLA PIETÀ (HALF 14TH CENTURY).

Particularly interesting are also the *chartae lapidariae* i.e. the trascription and public exposure on stone of some documents from notaries or chanceries.

Funerary inscriptions

These have various levels of complexity: some display only the name of the deceased, as the 15th century inscriptions of *Oddariello Boccazzola*, originally hanging in the nave of the Basilica di Santa Cecilia in Trastevere in Rome, today placed in the porch (D'Achille 1987: 80).

Some also display the name of the commissioner and/or the profession or other details about the deceased. More complex ones include epitaphs of literary or moral nature: two examples are the so called *Lapide dei fratelli Lercari* (Genua, 1259), and the tomb commissioned by Francesco Roncaglia (Modena, 1396), both of which are biligual and use the text in Latin to offer details on the lives of the deceased and the part in the vernacular to 'talk' to passers by and deliver moral messages of general importance.

FIGURE 3. ROME, CHURCH OF S. CECILIA, INSCRIPTION OF ODDARIELLO BOCCAZZOLA (14TH CENTURY)

The Genua stone reads: + *m°c°c°l°viiii ad dies xvi / agusti ante te/rcia transieru/ nt d(e) ho(c) s(e)c(u)lo domin/a Simoneta (et) Pre/civari(us) Lercari(us) ei(us) / frater q(u)e anime i(n) pace re/q(u)iescant ante deun ame(n). / Tu qi q(u)i ne t(r)ovi, p(er) De no me movi* (Stussi 1997: 152);[2] the Modena inscription remembers first Francesco Roncaglia as the commisioner of the tomb: *Hoc sepulcrum / fecit fieri Francis/cus filius q(uon)d(am) S(er) / Jacob(i) de Roncaleis / civius Mutin(ensis) de cinq(uan)/ti(n)a Sante Agathe / p(ro) se et suis her(e)dib(us) / MCC[CL] XXXXVI* and further combines an address to the passer by in the vernacular: *Eio fue quelo ch(e) / tu e e tu sera quelo / ch(e) e sum mi la mo/rte saspeta ognidi p(re)ga dio p(er) mi ch(e) eio / lo p(re)garo p(er) ti* (Giordani and Paolozzi Strozzi: 391-392).

Commemorative inscriptions

The third sub-category includes inscriptions intended to commemorate events or activities deemed as important for the life and history of a community. Such

---

[2] Formerly at the Chiesa di san Giovanni di Prè, today preserved at the Museo di Sant'Agostino, Genua.

FIGURE 4. MODENA, MUSEO LAPIDARIO ESTENSE, INSCRIPTION OF FRANCESCO RONCAGLIA (1396)

inscriptions always include the date, the name of the patron being celebrated, and of course the description of the event to be remembered.

To this category belong, for example, the inscription remembering the overflow of the river Arno in 1333: *Mcccxxxiii di quatro di novembre, giuovedì / la nocte poi vegnendo-l venerdì/ fu alta l'acqua d'Arno infino a qui* (Niccolai 1995: 14); or the inscription recording the consecration of a chapel preserved in the Church of San Gavino, in San Gavino Monreale in 1388: *Anno d(o)m(ini) m(illesi)mo CCCLXXXVIII lunis a die xxv / de S(an)c(t)o Saduru fudi in custa ecclesia fradi Fransciscu / Vasanelu ev(iscov)u de Terralba cu lu derivadu romua/n m[.]sua cio est calonigu Joh(ann)i de Lacu(n) calonigu de / Guspini verdi Julianu d'Oruu vi(r)di Mateu lora vi(r)di /Salbadori Colu vi(r)di Nigola de Lacu(n) in sa s(an)ta die bene / edifiche(n)di cuscus tres altari scio est s.altari de / mesu est dificadu at hunore de d(eu)s et de [sancta] / Maria et de s(an)c(t)u Gavini et Prontu ed Janu[ariu] / et s(an)c(t)u Miali in s.altari de destra s(an)c(t)u Augu[stinu] / [. . .]* (San Gavino 2013).

Most constituent elements of commemorative inscriptions can be found in the inscription visible in the left nave of the Church of Santo Stefano in Belluno which details date, commissioner and act to be remembered: *M°CCC°LXXXXVIIII° dì XV d(e) maço questo cimito(r)io e altar sì à fato far / iy comesari d(e) madona Katarina fiola che fo d(e) s(er) Bonifaci / d(e) Tiera p(er) la anema soa e d(e) iy so' mo(r)t* (Bertoletti 2006: 21).

Dedicatory inscriptions

The elements which are always present in such inscriptions are the name of the founder of the building, or the saint to which the building was dedicated, the artist responsible, the date and the commissioner. One of the most ancient texts from Belluno is an inscription of this kind, celebrating the dedication of a church to Sant'Andrea, originally hanging in the Church and now preserved at the Museo Civico in Belluno:

+ *In Chr(ist)i no(m)i(n)e am(en). Anno / d(omi)ni mcccl fata fo ques/sta glesia a onor de s(an)c(t)o / Andrea ap(osto)li, p(er) ord(e)nam(en)to d(e) / s(er) A(n)drea e Pero so fiol, de intro / glesia e fisla far dona / Bonavintura muier che fo / del dito Pero* (Stussi 1980: 95-96).

Captions and explanatory notes

Captions and in general detailed explanations of the content of an image, as well as poetry combined with images or artists' signatures constitute an important percentage of public writing. They all combine word and image: the textual part may have either a simple informative function (the signature of an artists) or an artistic function (when prose or verses accompany the image), or even a moralizing or educational intent. Captions may therefore be further divided into three sub-categories: 1. signatures (including both artists' signatures on stone, plaster, canvass etc.; and the names of patrons); 2. captions (descriptive or 'artistic'); 3. Moralizing or educational messages.

Let us consider, for example, the *Lastra del cavaliere Filippo Desideri*, found on the south end of the cloister of San Domenico in Bologna, now at the Museo Civico Medievale: *Trevisano/ Erriguço / f.(=fece/fecit)* (Breveglieri 1993: 147; Breveglieri 1997: 77) or the signatures in Sicilian, painted by the three artists responsible for the decorations in the Sala Magna of Palazzo Chiaramonte, Palermo: *Mastru Simuni pinturi di Curiglu[ni], Mastru Chicu pinturi di Naro e Mastru [P]illirinu Darenu pigituri de Palermu* (Bologna 1975: 95).

More articulate is the text of the inscription on the lower part of the gold frame of the

FIGURE 5. BOLOGNA, BOLOGNA, MUSEO CIVICO MEDIEVALE, TOMBSTONE OF KNIGHT FILIPPO DESIDERI (1315)

Figure 6. Bologna, Bologna, Museo Civico Medievale, Tombstone of knight Filippo Desideri (1315) – particular.

Polittico dell'Assunta at the Pinacoteca nazionale in Siena (1479): *Sani Petri pi(n)xit questa tavola a fata fare suoro Batista di Benedeto de nobili da Litiano MXCCCCLXXVIIII* (Torriti 1980: 297-298).

In this same category we included also texts designed to explain or complete the message of the painting. These may be found in various types of cartouches which have the same role as rubrics in a manuscript (Brugnolo 1997: 320). The most ancient and perhaps most famous example is the *Iscrizione di San Clemente* in the Basilica of S. Clemente in Rome, datable to the second half of the 11th century in which – as if in a modern day comic strip – we have figures engaged in a dialogue: the soldiers and their commander speak in Roman vernacular: *Fàlite deretro colo palo, Carvoncelle! - Albertel, Gosmari, tràite! - Fili dele pute, tràite*, whereas the saint speaks Latin: *Duritiam cordis vestris saxa traere meruistis*. The scene gives an iconic representation of an episode from the life of the Saint (Raffaelli 1987: 35-66).

Similarly, the two *telamoni*, today visible at the bases of the two columns at the sides of the portal of the Chiesetta di Sant'Antonio in Civita Castellana, datable to

FIGURE 7. CIVITA CASTELLANA, CHURCH OF S. ANTONIO, CARIATIDE (12TH CENTURY)

the 12th century, display a dialogue in the vernacular between a female figure - *teneas / cati/ve a/iuta/me* – to which the male character visibly crushed by the effort of sustaining the column replies: *non / pos/sum / quia / crepo* (Cimarra *et al.* 2002: 66-67).

As regards educational messages of a moral nature, we may recall the bench in San Marco in Venice, on the exterior wall of the Tesoro della Basilica di San Marco, towards Palazzo Ducale - datable, probably, to the late 14th century - which bears an inscription inserted in a cartouche held by two *putti*: *L'om po' far e / diè inpensar / e vega quel/o che li pò in / inchontrar* (Stussi 1997: 157).

Graffiti and extemporaneous writings

The category grouping graffiti and other forms of 'extemporaneous writings' include writings which were intended for public exposure, but were executed, as if on the whim of a moment, with no mediation of sorts, no commissioning or care as regards *mise en page* and design (Tedeschi 2002: 565-566).

Graffiti usually have a private nature. According to Formentin they can be classified as follows:

1. Graffiti of a private nature containing some form of emotional message (graffiti *di carattere emotivo-conativo*);
2. Graffiti whose message, as an *aide-mémoire*, is directed to a group (graffiti *di carattere pratico*):

FIGURE 8. CIVITA CASTELLANA, CHURCH OF S. ANTONIO, CARIATIDE AND TELAMONE (12TH CENTURY)

FIGURE 9. VENICE, EXTERIOR WALL OF THE TESORO DELLA BASILICA DI SAN MARCO, BENCH IN SAN MARCO (LATE 14TH CENTURY)

3. Graffiti with a factual content, impersonal in their style (graffiti *di carattere memorialistico événementiel*);
1. Graffiti constitutionally linked to the material on which there are written, and executed to preserve memory of an act of private or public relevance (graffiti *di carattere performativo*) (Formentin 2012: 101).

To the first group pertain texts with an obscene content such as those which are to be found in the Tomba Bartoccini, at the Necropoli dei Monterozzi, in Tarquinia, near Rome, datable to the 13th century. See, e.g. the graffiti documenting a sexual act between *Meliosus* and *Maria de baligiu* performed against the will (*mal gradu*) of a certain Bernabo or Barnabo: *Ego Meliosus sì f[o]/teo in questa g[ro]/ta Maria / de baligiu . Fec[.] / {a malg} a mal gradu di B[.]rnabo* (Tedeschi 2012: 63-64, Tedeschi 2002, n. 16).

Another example comes from the walls of the *bottega Mazzaforte*, today in the Monastero di Sant'Anna, Foligno. Recently, in this home cum workshop, a mural was found, preserving a series of graffiti – notes and drawings of various kinds – probably executed between 1468 and 1476. Particularly interesting the following inscription, probably the recipe for some kind of ink: *Un'oncia de galla amaçata,*

/ meza honcia de gomma, / un quarto de iletuale una honcia / una folgletta de vino bianco (Benazzi 2010: 245-261).³

Inscriptions on object in everyday use

The category referes to a kind of 'ephemeral epigraphy' the most prone to consumption and loss. An important example of it is the Umbrian wafer form, today at the Museo Nazionale del Bargello in Florence (1471-1503).

Domestic utensils were present in other Italian regions, but in Umbria they had a high artistic quality, testified to by other similar objects all datable to roughly the same period and housed at the Museo Nazionale dell'Umbria in Perugia.

Exceptional examples of this type of inscriptions are the two so called *coperte Guicciardini* woven in Sicily at the end of the 14th century and preserved one at the Museo del Bargello in Florence and the other at the Victoria and Albert Museum in London. They narrate, respectively, episodes from the story of Tristan and of the Amoroldo – although the stories intersect. The texts are in gothic letterforms and in Sicilian (Rajna 1998: 1547-1614; Proto Pisani *et al.* 2010; Morelli 1921-2).

Just to give an essay of the kind of narration contained herewith the transcription of the eight textual units from the first blanket (Rajna 1998: 1557):

Comu Tristainu et Gu[v]irnal[i] si parteru da lu rre Feramonti.
Comu lu misageri è vinutu a Tristainu.
Comu Tristainu et Guvirnali so vinuti allu re Marcu.
Comu lu rre Marcu fechi cavalieri Tristainu
Comu Tristainu vai nella isola per cumbactiri locu.
Comu lu Amoroldu vai alla isolecta.
Comu lu Amoroldu cumbactiu cu Tristainu a c[a]vallu.
Comu Tristainu cumbactiu cullu Amoroldo et speciaru li lanci.

The London blanket contains 14 textual units, which read as follows (Rajna 1998: 1557):

Comu lu rre Languis manda per lu trabutu in Cornualia.
Comu li missagieri so vinuti allu rre Marcu per lu tributu di secti anni.
Comu lu rre Languis cumanda chi vaia lo osti [in] Cornuvalgia.
Comu lu Amoroldu fa bandiri lu osti in Cornuvalgia.
Comu lu Amoroldu fa suldari la genti.

---

³ In Appendice, a p. 261 Romano Cordella's diplomatic transcription of all the graffiti in the Mazzaforte buildings.

Comu lu Amoroldu vai in Cornuvalgia.
Comu lu Amoroldu è vinutu in Cornuvalgia cun xxxx galei.
Comu Tristainu dai lu guantu allu Amoroldu de la bataglia.
Comu Tristainu aspecta lu Amoroldu alla isola dilu maru Sança Vintura.
Comu Tristainu bucta la varca arretu intu allu maru.
Comu lu infa de lu Amoroldu aspectava lu patrunu.
Comu Tristainu feriu lu Amorolldo in testa.
Comu lu Amoroldu feriu Tristainu a tr[a]dimentu.
Sitati de Irlanda.

The blankets were intended for the Tuscan Guicciardini family, and yet they were written in Sicilian. Was it because Sicilian vernacular carried sufficient literary prestige to warrant its use also outside of Sicily? Or because it was somehow linked to the genre of the narration? Or because the text did not really matter, but what mattered was the virtuoso exercise in producing such exceptional objects?

A similar quantity and variety of materials demonstrates in a somehow self-evident fashion the need for a flexible database.

We have decided to mark up the material according to an XML (eXtensible Markup Language) syntax capable of classifying the inscriptions according to their function.

Our "xml.function" file looks like this:

```xml
<?xml version="1.0" encoding="UTF-8"?>
<list>
    <item xml:id="PublicNotices">
        <term xml:lang="it">Public Notices</term>
    </item>
    <item xml:id="Normative">
        <term xml:lang="it"> Normative </term>
    </item>
    <item xml:id="Funerary">
        <term xml:lang="it"> Funerary </term>
    </item>
    <item xml:id="Commemorative ">
        <term xml:lang="it"> Commemorative </term>
    </item>
    <item xml:id="Dedicatory">
        <term xml:lang="it"> Dedicatory </term>
    </item>
    <item xml:id=" Caption">
```

```
                    <term xml:lang="it"> Caption </term>
            </item>
            <item xml:id="Signatures">
                    <term xml:lang="it"> Signatures </term>
            </item>
            <item xml:id=" ExplanatoryNotes ">
                    <term xml:lang="it"> Captions and explanatory notes
                    </term>
            </item>
            <item xml:id=" MoralizingEducational ">
                    <term xml:lang="it">Moralizing or educational
                    message </term>
            <item xml:id=" GraffitiExtemporaneousWritings ">
                    <term xml:lang="it"> Graffiti and extemporaneous
                    writings </term>
            </item>
            <item xml:id=" InscriptionsObjectEverydayUse">
                    <term xml:lang="it"> Inscriptions on object in
                    everyday use</term>
            </item>
</list>
```

We can interrogate the corpus on various levels - by obtaining a complete list of inscriptions according to type, or material, or language, or else by interrogating across such categories. Given the variety of the data inserted the potential for such interrogations is immense.

Linguistic Variety

The inscriptions are arranged according to modern administrative regions (Lombardia, Lazio, Molise, Apulia etc.). Each region hosts inscriptions in different vernaculars, alphabets and at times even literary languages (old French, Catalan, Sardinian).[4] There is also a significant number of bilingual and multilingual inscriptions and – even within the same vernaculars – very different levels of execution or sociolinguistic varieties. See, for example, the 13th century epitaph for Martinello di Rainone in octosyllabes in Old French which is inscribed in the Basilica dei Santi Felice e Fortunato in Vicenza: *Humiliteç e pacience / guit l<o>m<e> a Deu et astinence. / Martinel de Rainon ci gist / q'en sa vie ces rimes fist* (Morlino 2014: 25; Viscardi 1940: 261), or the frescoes of

---

[4] The issue is theoretically (and even practically) very complex. For the sake of simplicity we call here 'vernaculars' any of the languages which are not immediately classifiable in any greater detail, and 'languages' such 'vernaculars' endowed with a literary tradition or charged with a symbolic identity – such as e.g. Sardinian.

the *Fontana di Giovinezza*, *Prodi and Eroine* in the Sala Baronale at the Castello della Manta (Piccat 1992: 175-207) in Cuneo, or else the French *tituli* which accompany the *Età dell'uomo* in Palazzo Trinci, Foligno (Caciorgna 2001: 401-426). In Southern Italy we found inscriptions in Old French on the tomb of the Admiral Ludovico Aldemoresco, sculpted by Antonio Baboccio da Piperno in 1421, now in the Chiesa di San Lorenzo in Naples, which also carry a portion of text in Latin (De Blasi 1997: 269-271). The French text reads: *Ci demostre coment ardit et nobles ciavalier miser Lois moriske lassa sa gens tutts disconforte et ale con li anglies de diu e li montrer la gloria de le S. Paradis* and *Ci voit comant sant ayme et s. anton portent le n. princes et posciant roy Landislaus de duras et portet a soy les ardis et potens ciavaliers miser lois de moriske li presentent a la virgo Maria et son fius ihesu Xpiste in nel gloria del paradis ou le sant cecile et katerini demorent*. The intereference of an 'Italian' vernacular in the text is evident; but the French was probably used to mark the link between the Angiou family and the Aldemorescos (De Blasi 1997: 270-271).

Alfredo Stussi pointed out that the parallel use of Latin and vernacular could be considered as 'un riflesso dell'analoga alternanza presente da alcuni secoli in documenti mediolatini condizionati da una situazione di diglossia senza bilinguismo' (Stussi 1997: 152; Cannata 2016). As Stussi himself observed, the two parts must not be separated, but are to be considered as a unit and published as such. A bilingual inscription (Latin/ vernacular) walled into the exterior of a house in Via Giovanni da Verrazzano in Florence, keeps memory of a trip to Rome for the 1300 Jubilee made by a certain Ugolino together with his wife: *Ad perpetua(m) memoria(m) patea/t om(n)ib(us) evident(er) hanc paginam i/nspecturis q(uod) o(mn)ipote(n)s Deus i(n) an(n)o / d(omi)ni n(ost)ri (Iesu) (Christi) MCCC specialem g/r(ati)am co(n)tulit (christi)anis Samsepulcr/u(m) q(uo)d exstiterat a Saracenis ocu/patu(m) reco(n)victu(m) e(st) a Tartaris (et) (ch/risti)anis restitutu(m) (et) cu(m) eodem an<n>o f/uisset a papa Bonifatio sollepnis / remissio o(mn)ium peccator(um) videlic/et culpar(um) (et) penar(um) om(n)ib(us) eu(n)ti/b(us) Roma(m) indulta m(u)lti ex ip(s)is Tar/taris ad dicta(m) indulgentia(m) Rom/am accesserunt e andovi Ugoli/no chola molgle* (Gramigni 2012: 240). The main text is in a solemn (if garbled) Latin, whereas the actual event that Ugolino wished to be known slips out of the stone in a more current vernacular (Gramigni 2012: 88). The choice of language, as in the other cases already discussed, depends on the nature of the message to be conveyed.

Paradigmatic examples to test the potential of a database intending to allow for a detailed linguistic classification of medieval vernaculars is constituted by Sardinian inscriptions written in Sardinian, Gallurese, Catalan as well as continental Italian vernaculars. One of the most ancient Sardinian inscriptions, from the façade of the Santa Chiara cathedral in Iglesias, is in Tuscan. It is now preserved at the Istituto Minerario Giorgio Asproni, and reads (Sanna 2012: 2): [---] / [---] / *[lo magnifico signore] / [messer Petro Canino] / [podesta p(er) lo signore re e] / [domi]no [conte*

Ugolino di] / [Donerat]ico [signore de la] / [sexta] parte de lo [re]gno / [di Ka] llari e ora p(er) la Dio gra[tia] / p[odesta] di Pisa existen[t]e / [Petro di B]ernardo operaio (Serra and Tasca 1985). It had a Latin twin, with a nearly identical text. Both are datable between 1284 and May 1288. The commissioner of both – the Lord of Iglesias – was 'podestà' a high officer in Pisa.

On the right wall of the Cappella del Rimedio in the Santa Maria Assunta cathedral in Oristano there is a marble inscription which carries an epitaph, in Sardinian, for Filippo Mameli, a man of law, son of the canon Mariano Mameli: *Iobia ad dies VIII de maiu / de MCCCXLIX morivit messer / Philipo Mameli dotore de decre/tu et de lege et canonicu d'Arbar[ea] et iaghet cughe sossa sua* (Tasca 1986: 62). He must have played a significant role in the compilation of the law canon today known as the *Carta de Logu*. The date is given according to the Pisa style and corresponds to the 8th May 1348 (Tasca 1986: 62; Bonu 1973: 74).

In the church of San Gavino in San Gavino Monreale (Medio Campidano, south of Oristano) there is another inscription in Sardinian, particulary important because of its length. It records the date, 25th November 1387, when the bishop of Ales, Francesco Pasarino, came to the church to bless its chapel: *An(n)o d(omi)ni m(illesi) mo CCCLXXXVIII lunis a die XXV / de S(an)c(t)o Saduru fudi in custa ecclesia fradi Fransciscu / Vasanelu ev(iscov)u de Terralba cu lu derivadu romua / m sua cio est canoligu Joh(ann)i de Lacu(n) calongiu de / Guspini verdi Julianu d.Oruu vi(r)di Mateu lora vi(r)di / Salbadori Colu vi(r)di Nigola de Lacu(n) in sa s(an) ta die bene / edifiche(n)di cuscus tres altari scio est s.altari de / mesu est dificadu at hunore de d(eu)s et de [sancta] / Maria et de s(an)c(t)u Gavini et Prontu ed Janu[ariu] / et s(an)c(t)u Miali in s.altari de destra s(an)c(t)u Augu[stinu]/ [...]* (Serra 2013).

Near Sassari there are two inscriptions in Catalan and one in Gallurese, a most rare occurrence which is datable probably around 1445 to 1470, and is walled on the exterior of the apse of the Romanic church in Santa Vittoria del Sassu, Perfugas: *operaiu / malu / e fo/ra l'eremita* (Maxia 1999: 66). The person who commissioned the stone probably wanted to exclude the *operaiu malu e* i.e. the 'bad administrator' from the administration of the church's assets (Maxia 1999). Pietro Marras (Marras 1989) remarked that the definition of the language is a very thorny issue in this particular inscription: the article *l(u)* is Gallurese, *fora* is an adverb used in Corsica (but also pan-Italian) *operaiu* derives in all likelihood from the Tuscan *operaio* < OPERARIU(M) (with preservation of intertonic *-er-* as in Tuscan, whereas in Gallurese *-er-* develops in *-ar-*), and *e* for 'è' is of course pan-Italian (Maxia 1999).

There is an inscription in Catalan in the cloister of the Franciscan convent annexed to the church of Santa Maria di Betlem in Sassari which carries an epitaph for the dead Guilalmona, wife of the late Berengario: *Ací iau dona /Guilalmona mu/ler +i (?) fo / Be(re)n/garo / Gui/lar(t?)* (vel *Gui/lar(amon)?*) (Piras 2005: 39; Piras 2002: 84). The inscription is a precious document of the Catalan presence in Sassari between the third decade of the 14th and the beginning of the 15th centuries, as well as being a rare example of a funerary inscription in Catalan (with some interference of continental Italian vernaculars such as the final –o in the name) (Piras 2005: 5-6; Piras 2002: 87).

As suggested by the examples, determining the language of an inscription produced in Medieval Italy is no easy task. The identification of specific graphic, phonological, morphological and lexical features to guide the codification of the text, as well as the contextualization of the linguistic phenomena observed are all necessary to the task of their digitalization.

If we were to interrogate the database in search of the occurrences of the name *Ioachim, Gioachino, Ioachino* and derivatives in the captions of the *Storie di Maria* painted at the end of the 15th century by Andrea Delitio in the Basilica of Santa Maria Assunta in Atri (Matthiae and Trubiani 1976) the database would return the following results:

Quando **Ioacim** *<f>{i}ao cachiato de{he}<l>o tempio{ih}*
Quando **Iohaccim** *andò allu diserto   [...]*
Quando **Iohaccim** *se scontrò cu Anna ad Ort'Aura*

The name derives for the Hebrew *Yohaqim*, is *Ioakím* in Greek and *Ioachim* in Latin, but – as seen, it comes in a variety of forms (Rossebastiano and Papa 2005). The same applies to *Raniero* in the eight graffiti of the Tomba Bartoccini (13th century), which appears in Latin and the vernacular both with and without diphtongation (Tedeschi 2012:43-45, 46-47, 55-57; Formentin 2012: 95-113).

Foteo questa / g[r]ota / **Ranierius** *s[ì f]oteo questa / grota*
Ranerius/ *ic foteo bel/ horrore*
Sì foteo questa grota f(rate) / **Raineri Ranierius** *O(rdinis) Tem(pli)*

We may want to find all the occurrences of the grapheme <ç> in Roman inscriptions, a search which would return the following results, four from the 14th and one from the beginning of the 15th century (D'Achille 1987: 80, 83, 91, 75-76, 97-98):

Oddariello **Bocchaçiola**
Rienço Iordaniello
Rienço Ian(n)ipaolo

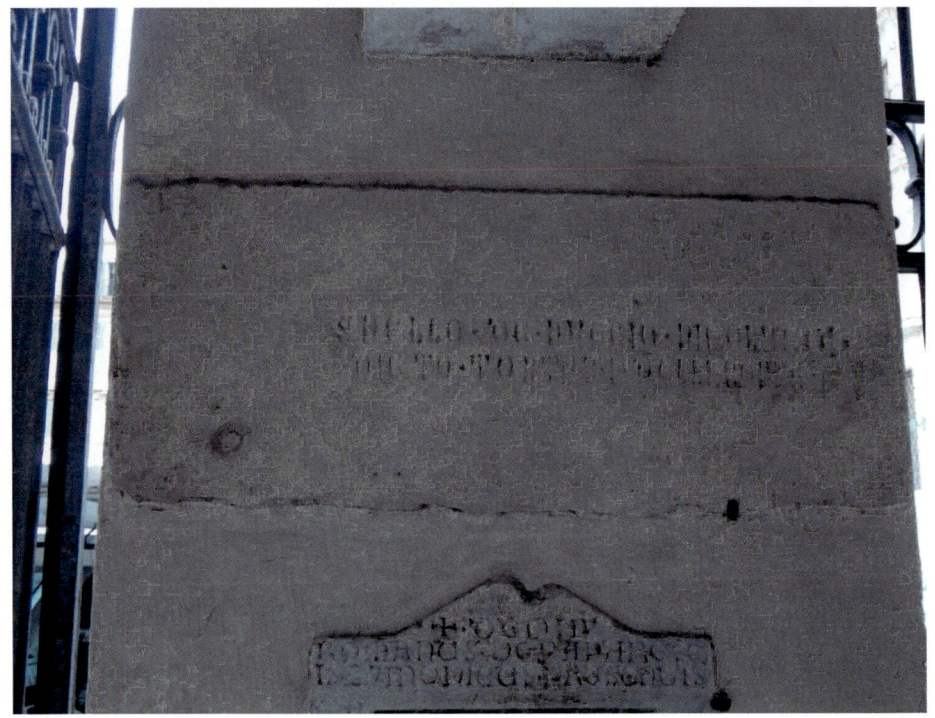

FIGURE 10. ROME, CHURCH OF S. MARIA IN TRASTEVERE, INSCRIPTION OF ANELLO DETTO TORTORA (BEGINNING OF 15TH CENTURY)

*In no(m)i(n)e D(omi)ni Ame(n). An/no D(omi)ni M(illesimo) CCC° LXV dello / mese de otrodo. / Madonna Margarit/a delli **Voccamaç/çi** monaca de s(an)c(to) / Sisto fece fare q/uessta colon(n)a p(er) l'/ anima de Ciecco **Voccama/ço** Anello de Nuccio **Nicolucca** / dicto Tortora delli Rofini.*

In *Rienço* and *Voccamaço* the grapheme <ç> should stand for [ts]; but the case of *Bocchaçiola* is less straightforward: [ts] or [tʃ]? In *Nicolucca* there is no cedille, but we probably should imagine <çç> as the intended writing. But there again <çç> stood for [ts] or [tʃ]? We might find an answer to these questions if we are to consider – and our database should enable us to – a greater number of occurrences.

The complexity of the languages present in the database forced us to devise some fixed leves of interrogation. We decided on three: area of origin; linguistic analysis and intertextual links within the corpus. Each item must be classified according to linguistic area, and we used the following tags: Franco provençal; Provençal; German; Ladino; Slovene; Friulan; Venetian: (Venice, Hinterland); Gallo-italic (Emiliano, Ligure, Lombardo, Piemontese,

Romagnolo, Marchigiano); Tuscan (north, central, south); Rome; Area mediana (Lazio, Umbria, Marche, Abruzzi); South I (Abruzzi, Molise, Campania, Apulia-North, Marche); South II (Salento, Calabria-South, Sicily, other); Sardinian (Logudoro, Campidano); Sassari; Gallura; Latin (for multilingual inscriptions only).

The second level deals with graphic, phonological, morphological, syntactic and lexical features in the text which are then used to determine the 'language' of the inscription, which is often independent of the area of production. The third level concerns tags which will allow to create links between documents presenting similar features, thus creating a network of intertextual links. The codification of all the words present in the corpus, together with the graphemes, phonemes (and sounds) which is possible in EpiDoc XML will allow us to create automatic indexes for all nouns (antroponyms, toponyms etc.) and all the linguistic forms we deemed as relevant.

This will allow for the creation of indexes which will constitute precious repertoires of unpublished materials relating to Italian medieval vernaculars.

Issues in the digitization of epigraphic material

How to publish inscriptions featuring in complex iconographic constructions

Our corpus contains several inscriptions which are part of multiple scenes – generally frescoes adorning different walls of a hall – the interpretation of which is not easy or, indeed, straightforward.

Sometimes it is difficult to reconstruct the intended sequence of the scenes, which allows for different interpretations of the text – be it a narration, or captions, proverbs, dialogues etc. Such is the case of the Trecento fresco of the *Scala Santa col Trionfo della Morte* preserved at the Sacro Speco in Subiaco, where Death – a skeleton with a big mane of hair – rides a white horse brandishing in its right hand a sword (D'Achille 2012a: 45-50). Under the horse corpses are visible. On the right there are 4 destitute characters among which a bearded old man and an elderly lady. On the left there are two young men, expensively dressed, one of which holds a falcon in his hand and is caught in the instant in which Death pierces him through the neck with the sword. The fresco is accompanied by a rich textual apparatus, unfortunately almost illegible: it is constituted by the dialogues the artists imagined exchanged in the scene, and therefore the script appears near the mouths of the featured characters. The attributions, however, are far from clear, and the proposed interpretations vary greatly. Here the transcription of the text (D'Achille 2012a: 56-57):

La Morte:
I' sò colei c'ocide omne persona,
giovane e vecchia, né verun ne lasso:
de grande altura subito l'abbasso.
Tu lasse noi che sempre te chiamemo
desiderando che ne dea la morte
[... < -orte >]
I due giovani:
Changiato sé nel viso [...]
[...] tanto scolorito;
vorria sapere chi t'à così ferito.
Cho[n] gran dolor e con forti sospiri   10
sentia la morte che ferì al core;
de subito ne tolse omne valore.
Mors malis formidabilis et bonis desiderabilis, nemini evitabilis.

Simpler, but no less interesting is the *Incontro dei Vivi e dei Morti* from the church in the San Paolo cemetery in Poggio Mirteto, near Rome, edited by Paolo D'Achille (2012b). The fresco is divided into two parts: on the left features a crowned man on a horse and on the right three decomposing corpses. The inscription, now illegible, counts ten rhyming verses painted between the horse's legs, and reads (D'Achille 2012b: 36-38):

FIGURE 11. SUBIACO, SACRO SPECO, FRESCO OF SCALA SANTA WITH TRIONFO DELLA MORTE (14TH CENTURY)

FIGURE 12. SUBIACO, SACRO SPECO, FRESCO OF SCALA SANTA WITH TRIONFO DELLA MORTE (14TH CENTURY) – PARTICULAR 1.

FIGURE 13. SUBIACO, SACRO SPECO, FRESCO OF SCALA SANTA WITH TRIONFO DELLA MORTE (14TH CENTURY) – PARTICULAR 2.

La vita m'è scura
la morte dura.
Perdutu aio risu e gioia.
Iocu e alegretia no m'e(n)voglia.
No me cosegliate 5
cosa ke si' falace,
c'a Deu me so' re(n)nutu
ca li ò petutu.
Male n[o v]oglio fare,
[ec]cu me vo [...<are>]. 10

There are traces of another text, presumably in Latin, above the three corpses, possibly to be attributed to the corpses themselves, whereas the text in the vernacular is to be ascribed to the knight (D'Achille 2012b: 43).

FIGURE 14. POGGIO MIRTETO, CHURCH OF S. PAOLO, INCONTRO DEI VIVI E DEI MORTI
(14TH CENTURY)

FIGURE 15. POGGIO MIRTETO, CHURCH OF S. PAOLO, INCONTRO DEI VIVI E DEI MORTI (14TH CENTURY) – PARTICULAR 1.

Paradigmatic for its complexity is the text which accompanies the *Trionfo della Morte* and the *Danza Macabra* from Clusone, near Bergamo, dated 1485 (Frugoni 1979). Most of the text went lost over time. Many scholars have studied this document: Astorre Pellegrini in 1978 produced a fac-simile and dated the inscription; Arsenio Frugoni edited the text and Luisa Tognoli Bardin provided a new transcription (Pellegrini 1978: 19; Tognoli Bardin 1986: 188-196). The following is Frugoni's edition (1979: 221, 227, 235-6):

Death carries two inscriptions:

[1] Left:
Gionto per nome chamata morte
ferischo a chi tocharà la sorte;
non è homo chosí forte
che da mi non pò schapare

[2] Right:
Gionto la morte piena de equaleza,
sole voi ve volio e non vostra richeza
e digna sonto da portar corona 3
perché signorezi ognia persona.

Further inscriptions:

[3]
Chi è fundato in la iustitia e [bene]
e lo alto Dio non discha[ro tiene]
la morte a lui non ne vi[en con dolore] 3
poy che in vita [lo mena ass]a[i meliore]

[4]
Ognia omo more e questo mondo lassa
chi ofende a Dio amaramente passa.
1485 3

[5] Above the *Danza Macabra*:
O ti che serve Dio del bon core
non havire pagura a questo ballo venire,
ma alegramente vene e non temire, 3
poy chi nase elli convene morire.

[6]:
Son fine [---] timeamus superbia avarizia ira

The above are only a few of the numerous examples of this types of inscriptions and of the problems they pose. We should perhaps also recall the already mentioned inscription of San Clemente (11th century, Raffaelli 1987), or the captions in the frescoes of santa Francesca Romana in the Monastero delle Oblate di Tor de Specchi (D'Achille 1987a), both in Rome; as well as the text accompanying the *Maestà* by Simone Martini (Brugnolo 1987) or the frescoes of the *Buono e Cattivo Governo* by Ambrogio Lorenzetti in the Palazzo Pubblico in Siena (Brugnolo 1995), all cases which pose complex issues for the edition of the text and the attribution of the dialogues.

The intimate connections between texts and images make it nearly impossible to provide a diplomatic edition of the text which could claim to reproduce its original format, not to mention the difficulties in reading texts which are written on ceilings and dark corners of high walls, or on deteriorating plaster. We have introduced a section of *Notes* to provide all the necessary information to complement the transcripton and clarify the nature of the texts transcribed.

As regards the critical edition, there will be a critical apparatus and a field for comments, to give information on previous editions of the text or discuss alternative readings. The database is not designed to replace other more traditional forms of editing, but to function as an orderly archive for all the information available to date (information which can be easily updated as other data or studies become available) and cater for the needs of scholars in different fields.

Each entry will have the edition of the text, a diplomatic transcription, critical apparatus, commentary, images, and naturally an updated bibliography.

Other issues and some proposed solutions

It is often necessary, in order to reconstruct a text now barely legible or, worse, partially destroyed, to make use of secondary sources, and wherever possible, photographic reproductions. A photographic apparatus is essential and constitutes one of the aims of the project. However, images and photographic metadata are not always available either because of copyright issues, but more often because of the lack of good images and sometimes because of the impossibility for us to make them specially.

Available images of painting, however excellent in quality, very often cut out the script, considered accessory. Such is the case for the captions of the fresco in the *Storie di S. Aldebrando* from Fossombrone, Marche. The painting, by Antonio Alberti da Ferrara (15th century) occupies two thirds of the left wall of a chapel of the ancient Cathedral in Fossombrone. The top end of the wall is dedicated to the *Adoration of the Magi*, the lower part is divided into four little porches each featuring an episode from the life of the Saint (the resurrection of the partridge; the miracle of the cherries; the healing of the obessed; the Saint's death) above each of them, captions in contemporary gothic script are inscribed:

[1] *Amalato a morte ghe fo p(re)xentata una perdixe cota recordandosi ch(e) no h [...?]*

comandò alla p(er)dixe ch(e) se ne andasse alla foresta e p(rese)nte loro lì se ne vollò.

[2] *poi . . . ghe domandò de le cierexe et essi tatievano p(er) co(m)passione ch'hera de gienaro coma<n>dò ch(e) gisseno al albero dove ello hera uxato de dire mesa e andato trovoghene e p(or)t{r}oghene.*

[3] *Qomo molti amalati d'Anchona e d'altri lochi demoniati e xpiritati e de diverse mallati[e] facendoghe el signo dela santa crocie per la posanca de Dio liberati se partiano.*

[4] *Como quando el morì tre campane ch erano in sullo campanile del vescovo sonono ttanto da per se instese como se sona per haltri morti.*

The inscriptions, now lost, are recorded in copper incisions made in the 1820s (Colasanti 1915: 368).

More frequently texts are preserved in manuscripts. Such is the case of the ex-voto from Scicli, near Ragusa in Sicily, in the church of Santa Maria della Croce. There are six frames on two levels illustrating some of the miracles of Santa Maria della Croce in Sicilian vernacular. One of them is only readable in a manuscript transcription (Drago and Nifosì 1976: 61).

[1] *Comu sedu mucicatu di cani araiatu u frusteri fu minatu S. M. di la Cruchi apasi . P. Caminu. fu sanu.*

[2] *Comu. sedu. lu. patri. Fra. Ivani. P. Mari. si Victiru. anigati li marinari. prigadu. S. M. de la Cruchi. foru. libri.*

[3] *Comu. A. Terranova. fu. Firutu u. garzuni acumadausi. S. M. de la Cruchi. fu. libru*

[4] *Comu. una. dona. avia. lu. mali. de. chacu. p. virtuti di S. M. di. la Cruchi. fu. sana.*

[5] *Co. certi. doni. avedu. li. filii. malati. X. e vinendu. A. S. M. de. la Cruchi. furunu. sani.*

[6] *comu. fr. glu. dagilu. mavtisi. sautau. di. na… S. M. di. la. Cruchi. e. fu. sanu. di. la. gula. I. chitormu. L…* (Drago and Nifosì 1976: 65).

When marking up in EpiDoc n. [6], we shall proceed as follows:

> <supplied reason="undefined" evidence="previouseditor"> Comu fr glu dagilu mavtisi sautau di na S. M. di la Cruchi e fu sanu di la gula I chitormu L </supplied>

The marking up of the missing text is recognizable through the element <supplied> specified by the attributes (*reason* ed *evidence*) which allow us to markup the text as 'text visible to previous editor, but now lost'. When applying this markup to the style sheet XSLT and the file is transformed in HTML then the text will appear as follows or with some other style designed to single it out.

<u>Comu fr glu dagilu mavtisi sautau di na S. M. di la Cruchi e fu sanu di la gula I chitormu L.</u>

If in Scicli only a small part of the text is lost, the inscriptions about the origins of Rome from Palazzo Trinci in Foligno are mostly lost, with only a few fragments extant. The text, originally made up of nine stanzas, is now readable in the third and parts of the fourth stanza (figure 16-17).

We have, however, a record of the whole poem, the transcription provided by Ludovico Iacobilli, a 17th century scholar (Caciorgna 2001: 401-406):

Diplomatic edition

>[3]
>PER PIETA SONPO[ ] PRESSO AL FIUME
>   ]OLO (ET) REMO ALLA FORTUNA DATJ
>DOVE PIU GIORNI FORON NUTRICHATI
>DAUNA LUPA PER HUMAN COSTUME
>
>[4]
>SI CHOME [
>YLYA DOPO [
>[   ]
>PER OBSERVARSE [   ]GGE.

FIGURE 16. FOLIGNO, PALAZZO TRINCI. MUSEO DELLA CITTÀ, LOGGIA DI ROMOLO E REMO, STORIES OF ROMULUS AND REMUS (1411-1412).

Figure 17. Foligno, Palazzo Trinci. Museo della città, Loggia di Romolo e Remo, Stories of Romulus and Remus (1411-1412) - particular.

Critical edition

    [1]
Intra Vestali virgini se noma   1
Ilia nata da re Nomitore,
La quale de Marte per venereo ardore   3
Concepì i fondatori dell'alma Roma.

    [2]
Gravida fatta poi in doi figlioli,
Per infamia fugire del grave incesto,
Commanda che sien posti in loco alpestro   6
De notte tempo, con gran pianto e doli.

    [3]
Per pietà son posti presso al fiume
Romolo et Remo, alla fortuna dati,   9
Dove più giorni foron nutrichati
Da una lupa per human costume.

[4]
Sì chome nella historia se legge,　　　　12
Ylya dopo el parto è sepellita
Viva in tal modo che priva de vita
Per observarse la severa legge.

[5]
Per Faustolo regio pastore furon portati　　15
Li dui infanti ad Accha Laurenza
Sua donna qual, per sua gran clemenza,
Fine all'adulta etate ha nutricati.　　　　18

[6]
Surgon come pastori Romolo e Remo
Tirando dietro a sé simile gente
Et, poi che fatti son ciascun possente,　　21
Feceono alcuno de soe robbe scemo.

[7]
Romolo et Remo colla voglia ardita,
Con turma de pastori ciascuno armato,　　24
Intraro in Alba et levaron de stato
Avuncho Amulio et tolserli la vita.

[8]
Per haver la ciptade edificata,　　　　27
La quale sia magnifica e capace,
Ciascun consiglia, sì come li piace,
Et ch'ella sia da Romol nominata.　　　30

[9]
Quivi vedete sì come se mura
L'alma ciptà gloriosa e possente,
Qual fece tributorie l'altre gente　　　33
E quasi a tuto el mondo fe' paura

The stories on the origins of Rome are only one of the pictorial cycles painted for Palazzo Trinci, for which a complex and rich iconographic programme was devised in the years 1411-1412. Alongside the stories of Romulus and Remus there are the *Uomini famosi*, the *Arti Liberali* and *Filosofia*, the three versions of the *Sette età dell'Uomo*, the *Ore del Giorno*, the *Nove Prodi* and the *Storie di Maria*. They are all accompanied by *tituli* in three languages; Latin, Old French, Italian vernacular. How to account for them both individually and as a unit? How to avoid tearing off from their context the individual components of a pictorial cycle?

To solve the problem we are tagging the inscriptions according to <placeName/> and <origPlace/> so that we will be able to find all frescoes located in the "Palazzo Trinci" which stands in Foligno.

We have also inserted an intertextual markup, linking through the tag <ref> all the frescoes, as in the followingEpiDoc string:

<ref target= "EDV0020">

In HTML this can look like this:

See also in the Sala delle Arti e dei Pianeti:

-(EDV0020) Vernacular tituli for the Arti Liberali
-(EDV0021) Vernacular tituli for the Età e delle Ore del giorno

See also in the Corridoio:

-(EDV0022) Vernacular tituli for the Età dell'uomo in Old French

EpiDoc allows us the flexibility we need for a digital edition of our database of vernacular inscription, written in languages without names and in varieties which defy any attempt of a rigid classification.

The Database template

1. Common identification and record number

The database will be searchable both through the number of a specific entry, and through its common denomination (e.g. Graffito di Commodilla; Iscrizione di San Clemente).

2. Measurements

3. Localization

For the purpose of localization, and for ease of consultation we have decided to use modern administrative regions (Lombardia, Lazio, Molise, Puglia etc.)

a) Origin
A drop-down menu will allow to state
Region where the item was produced (e.g. Marche)
Place (historical denomination – e.g. Sassoferrato)
Original Destination (e.g. Florence, Santa Maria del Fiore)

b) Conservation
Current location (e.g. Apulia)
Place (Modern city and country – if not in Italy - Institution, or street)

4. Geolocalization (latitude and longitude)

This will allow us to build – with time – interactive maps showing the context in which the inscriptions are preserved.

5. Type of Object

- Public Notices
  - *1.1 Normative inscriptions* (edicts, laws, etc.)
  - *1.2 Funerary inscriptions* (tombstones and other forms of remembrance)
  - *1.3 Monimenta* (memories of events, ex-voto etc.)
  - *1.4. Dedicatory inscriptions* (made as some form of acknowledgment for patronage)
- Captions and explanatory notes
  - Signatures
  - Explanatory captions in paintings, the most ancient and possibly famous of which is the strip in the Basilica si San Clemente, also one of the very first documents of an Italian vernacular
  - Messages of a didascalic or moralizing nature, such as proverbs
- Graffiti and other casual and unplanned writings
- Inscriptions on objects in everyday use

6. Material

- bronze
- copper
- plaster
- silver
- gold
- cloth
- clay, terracotta, ceramics
- iron
- stone
- wood
- marble
- mosaic
- lead
- glass
- canvas
- unknown

7. Preservation condition
State of conservation [drop down menu]

- good
- legible
- partially legible
- fragmentary

8. Fac-simile transcription

9. Critical edition / Apparatus

10. Script

11. Alphabet

12. Metre → si / no

13. Languages

This section has a drop-down menu, much more complex that the template we find in EDR which only allows for Latin, Greek, Bilingual Latin-Greek bilingual or other

    Linguistic Area → Menu on two levels

- Franco provençal
- provençal
- German
- Ladino
- Slovene
- Friulian
- Venetian
  - Venice
  - hinterland
- Gallo-italic
  - emiliano
  - ligure
  - lombardo
  - piemontese
  - romagnolo
  - marchigiano

- Tuscan
  - north
  - central
  - south
- Rome
- Area mediana
  - Latium
  - Umbria
  - Marche
  - Abruzzi
- South (I)
  - Abruzzi
  - Molise
  - Campania
  - Apulia (north)
  - Lucania
  - Calabria (north)
  - Marche
- South (II)
  - Salento
  - Calabria (south)
  - Sicily
  - other
- Sardinian
  - logudoro
- Sassari
- Gallura
- Campidano

14. Date

The four fields included in this section allow to limit the search exclusively to inscriptions' chronology, either entering the year (1), dates by quarter (2), half century (3), century (4) *termini ad* and *post quem* (5)

15. Image(s)

16. Audio

17. Comments

18. Bibliography

Bibliography

Benazzi, G. 2010. Un'insolita scoperta nel monastero: le case e le botteghe di dei Mazzaforte e dell'Alunno. In A. C. Filannino (ed.), *Il monastero di Sant'Anna a Foligno. Religiosità e arte attraverso i secoli*: 245-261. Foligno, Edizioni Orfini Numeister.

Bertoletti, N. 2006. Testi in volgare Bellunese del Trecento e dell'inizio del Quattrocento. *Lingua e stile* 41/1: 3-26.

Bologna, F. 1975. *Il soffitto della Sala Magna allo Steri di Palermo e la cultura feudale siciliana nell'autunno del Medioevo*. Palermo, Flaccovio.

Bonu, R. 1973 *Oristano nel suo Duomo e nelle sue chiese: cenni storici e due appendici*. Cagliari, STEF.

Breveglieri, B. 1993. *Scrittura e immagine: le lastre terragne del Medioevo bolognese*. Spoleto, Centro Italiano di Studi sull'Alto Medioevo.

Breveglieri, B. 1997. Il volgare nelle scritture esposte bolognesi. Memorie di costruzione ed opere d'arte. In Ciociola, C. (ed.) 1997. *Visibile parlare. Le scritture esposte nei volgari italiani dal Medioevo al Rinascimento*: 73-100. Napoli, Edizioni scientifiche italiane.

Brugnolo, F. 1987. Le terzine della "Maestà" di Simone Martini e la prima diffusione della "Commedia". *Medioevo romanzo* 12: 135-154.

Brugnolo, F. 1995. Le iscrizioni in volgare: testo e commento. In E. Castelnuovo (ed.), *Ambrogio Lorenzetti. Il Buon Governo*: 381-391. Milano, Electa.

Brugnolo, F. 1997. «Voi che guardate...». Divagazioni sulla poesia per pittura del Trecento. In Ciociola, C. (ed.) 1997. *Visibile parlare. Le scritture esposte nei volgari italiani dal Medioevo al Rinascimento*: 305-340. Napoli, Edizioni scientifiche italiane.

Cacchioli, L. and Tiburzi, A. 2014. Lingua e forme dell'epigrafia in volgare (secc. IX-XV). 1. Scrivere il volgare: su pietra, sui muri; 2. Esporre perché: tipologie e funzioni. *Studj Romanzi* 10: 311-352.

Cacchioli, L. and Tiburzi, A. 2014. Contributi e fonti per lo studio del volgare esposto in Italia. *Critica del testo* 18/2: 103-138.

Caciorgna, M. 2001. 'Sanguinis et belli fusor'. Contributo all'esegesi dei *tituli* di Palazzo Trinci (Loggia di Romolo e Remo, Sala delle Arti e dei Pianeti, Corridoio). In G. Benazzi and F. F. Mancini (eds.), *Il Palazzo Trinci di Foligno*: 401-426. Perugia, Quattroemme.

Cannata, N. 2014. Le Parole Sono Pietre: *Lingua Communis* e *Lingua Literata* in alcune epigrafi romane (secc. IV-VI). *Studj Romanzi* 10: 281-310.

Cannata, N. 2016 (in press). Lontano da dove? Tradizioni culturali e coscienza linguistica in Europa. *Studj Romanzi* 12: 2016, in print.

Cimarra, L., Condello, E., Miglio L., Signorini M., Supino P. and Tedeschi C. (eds.) 2002. *Inscriptiones Medii Aevi Italiae (Saec. VI-XII), LAZIO ~ Viterbo, 1*. Spoleto, Centro Italiano di Studi sull'Alto Medioevo.

Colasanti A. 1915. Contributo alla storia della pittura nelle Marche. *Biblioteca delle Arti* 9: 355-373.

D'Achille, P. 1987. Iscrizioni votive e sepolcrali in volgare nei secoli XIV-XVI. In F. Sabatini and S. Raffaeli and P. D'Achille (eds.), *Il volgare nelle chiese di Roma. Messaggi graffiti, dipinti e incisi dal IX al XVI secolo*: 69-107. Roma, Bonacci Editore.

D'Achille, P. 1987a. Le didascalie degli affreschi di Santa Francesca Romana (con un documento inedito del 1463). In F. Sabatini and S. Raffaeli and P. D'Achille (eds.), *Il volgare nelle chiese di Roma. Messaggi graffiti, dipinti e incisi dal IX al XVI secolo*: 108-183. Roma, Bonacci Editore.

D'Achille, P. 2012a. Le scritte in versi dell'affresco sublacense col Trionfo della Morte. In P. D'Achille (ed.), *Parole: al muro e in scena. L'italiano esposto e rappresentato*: 45-65. Firenze, Franco Cesati editore.

D'Achille, P. 2012b. Un affresco trecentesco laziale con una scritta volgare in versi: l'incontro dei vivi e dei morti di Poggio Mirteto, in D'Achille, P. (ed.), *Parole: al muro e in scena. L'italiano esposto e rappresentato*: 28-44. Firenze, Franco Cesati Editore.

De Blasi, N. 1997. Iscrizioni in volgare nell'Italia meridionale: prime esplorazioni. In Ciociola, C. (ed.) 1997. *Visibile parlare. Le scritture esposte nei volgari italiani dal Medioevo al Rinascimento*: 261-301. Napoli, Edizioni scientifiche italiane.

Drago G. and Nifosì, P. 1976. *Aspetti Storico-artistici della contea di Modica in Santa Maria della Croce di Scicli*. Ispica, Comune di Scicli.

Favreau, R. 1997. *Épigraphie médiévale*. Tutnhout, Brepols.

Formentin, V. 2012. I graffiti in volgare: uno studio filologico-linguistico. In C. Tedeschi (ed.), *Graffiti Templari. Scritture e simboli medievali in una tomba etrusca di Tarquinia*: 95-113. Roma, Viella.

Frugoni, A. 1979. I temi della Morte nell'affresco della Chiesa dei Disciplinati a Clusone. In Frugoni (ed.), *Incontri nel Medioevo*: 217-249. Bologna, il Mulino.

Giordani, N. and Paolozzi Strozzi, G. 2005. *Il museo lapidario estense, catalogo generale*. Venezia, Marsilio Editore.

Gramigni, T. 2012. *Iscrizioni medievali in territorio fiorentino fino al XIII secolo*. Firenze, Firenze University Press.

Johnson, M. 1987. *The Body in the Mind. The Bodily Basis of Meaning, imagination and reason*. Chicago, Chicago University Press.

Matthiae, G. and Trubiani, B. 1976. *Gli affreschi della cattedrale di Atri*. Roma, Autostrade S. p. a.

Marras, P. 1989. L'Anglona. In M. Brigaglia (ed.), *Le chiese nel verde: architetture religiose rurali nella provincia di Sassari*: 76-93. Sassari, Amministrazione provinciale, Assessorato alla cultura e pubblica istruzione.

Maxia, M. 1999. Un'antica epigrafe in gallurese. In M. Maxia (ed.), *Studi storici sui dialetti della Sardegna settentrionale*: pp. 55-90. Sassari, Studium.

Morelli, L. 1921-22. Un trapunto trecentesco. *Dedalo. Rassegna d'arte* 2: 770-83.

Morlino, L. 2014. Spunti per un riesame della costellazione letteraria franco-italiana. *Francigena* 1: 5-81, 25.

Niccolai, F. 1995. *Lapidi in Firenze. Storie e personaggi che hanno fatto grande questa città*. Firenze, Coppini.

Pellegrini, A. 1878. *Nuove illustrazioni sull'affresco del Trionfo e Danza della Morte in Clusone*. Bergamo, Gaffuri e Gatti.

Petrucci, A. 1997. Il volgare esposto: problemi e prospettive. In Ciociola, C. (ed.) 1997. *Visibile parlare. Le scritture esposte nei volgari italiani dal Medioevo al Rinascimento*: 45-58. Napoli, Edizioni scientifiche italiane.

Petrucci, L. 2010. *Alle origini dell'epigrafia volgare. Iscrizioni italiane e romanze fino al 1275*. Pisa, Edizioni Plus.

Piccat, M. 1992. Le scritte in volgare della fontana di Giovinezza, dei Prodi e delle Eroine. In G. Carità (ed.), *Le Arti alla Manta: il Castello e l'Antica Parrocchiale*: 175-207. Torino, Galatea.

Piras, G. 2002. Le epigrafi funerarie medievali della chiesa di S. Maria di Betlem in Sassari. *Biblioteca Francescana Sarda* 10: 69-93.

Piras, G. 2005. Inscriptiones Medii Aevi ecclesiarum Sassarensium (saecula XIII-XV). *Archivio Storico Sardo* 44: 359-422.

Proto Pisani, R. C., Ciatti, M., Conti, S. and Vaccari, M. G. 2010. *La "Coperta" Guicciardini. Il restauro delle imprese di Tristano*. Firenze, Edifir.

Raffaelli, S. 1987. Sull'iscrizione di San Clemente. Un consuntivo con integrazioni. In F. Sabatini and S. Raffaeli and P. D'Achille (eds.), *Il volgare nelle chiese di Roma. Messaggi graffiti, dipinti e incisi dal IX al XVI secolo*: 35-66. Roma, Bonacci Editore.

Rajna, P. 1998. Intorno a due antiche coperte, con figurazioni tratte dalle storie di Tristano e Isotta. In G. Lucchini (ed.), *Scritti di filologia e linguistica italiana e romanza*: 1547-1614. Roma, Salerno.

Rossebastiano A. and Papa E. 2005, *I nomi di persona in Italia. Dizionario storico ed etimologico*. Torino, UTET.

Sabatini, F. 1996. Voci nella pietra dall'Italia mediana. Analisi di un campione e proposte per una tipologia delle iscrizioni in volgare. In V. Coletti, R. Coluccia and P. D'Achile and N. De Blasi and L. Petrucci (eds.), *Italia linguistica delle Origini*: 569- 625. Lecce, Argo.

Sabatini, F. 1997. Voci nella pietra dall'Italia mediana. Analisi di un campione e proposte per una tipologia delle iscrizioni in volgare. In Ciociola, C. (ed.) 1997. *Visibile parlare. Le scritture esposte nei volgari italiani dal Medioevo al Rinascimento*: 177-222. Napoli, Edizioni scientifiche italiane.

Sanna, A. L. 2012. *Iglesias, chiesa di Santa Chiara (CI): scavi nella cattedrale di Ugolino della Gherardesca (2010-2011)* http://www.fastionline.org/docs/FOLDER-it-2012-263.pdf

Serra, A. 2013, *Le iscrizioni medievali di San Gavino* http://www.sangavinomonreale.net/2013/10/07/le-iscrizioni-medievali-di-san-gavino/

Serra, G. and Tasca, C. 1985. Epigrafi medioevali di Villa di Chiesa: note per la storia della città alle sue origini. In *Studi su Iglesias medioevale*: 271-285. Pisa, ETS.

Stussi, A. 1997. Epigrafi medievali in volgare dell'Italia settentrionale e della Toscana. In Ciociola, C. (ed.) 1997. *Visibile parlare. Le scritture esposte nei volgari italiani dal Medioevo al Rinascimento*: 150-175. Napoli, Edizioni scientifiche italiane.

Stussi, A. 1980. Antichi testi dialettali veneti. In M. Cortelazzo (ed.), *Guida ai dialetti veneti II*: 85-100. Padova, CLEUP.

Stussi, A. 1997. Epigrafi medievali in volgare dell'Italia settentrionale e della Toscana. In Ciociola, C. (ed.) 1997. *Visibile parlare. Le scritture esposte nei volgari italiani dal Medioevo al Rinascimento*: 150-175. Napoli, Edizioni scientifiche italiane.

Tasca, C. 1986. Le influenze pisane nella produzione epigrafica sarda e catalana del XIV secolo. *Archivio storico sardo* 35: 61-80.

Tedeschi, C. 2002. Contributo allo studio paleografico dei graffiti parietali latini. In F. Magistrale and C. Drago and P. Fioretti (eds.), *Libri, documenti, epigrafi medievali: possibilità di studi comparativi*: 565-585. Spoleto, Centro Italiano di Studi sull'Alto Medioevo.

Tedeschi, C. 2012. Le iscrizioni: edizione, analisi paleografica e commento. in C. Tedeschi (ed.), *Graffiti templari. Scritture e simboli medievali in una tomba etrusca di Tarquinia, Scritture e libri del medioevo*: 29-94. Roma, Viella.

Tognoli Bardin, L. 1986. Giacomo Borlone e Giacomo Busca. In F. Mazzini (ed.), *I pittori bergamaschi dal XIII al XIX secolo. Il Quattrocento I*: 188-196 Bergamo, Bolis.

Torriti, P. 1980. *La Pinacoteca nazionale di Siena. I dipinti dal XII al XV secolo.* Genova, Sagep.

Viscardi, A. 1940. Un epitaffio francese a Vicenza (sec. XIII). *Archivum Romanicum* 24: 285-300.

Signals, Symbols, and Spaces in the Ashmolean Latin Collection

Hannah Cornwell and Jane Masséglia
Ashmolean Latin Inscriptions Project, Oxford

The Rationale behind the AshLI project

The Ashmolean Latin Inscription Project (AshLI) is a three-way collaboration between the University of Warwick, the Centre for the Study of Ancient Document at the University of Oxford, and the Ashmolean Museum, and will run from 2013-2016 with support from the AHRC, under Principal Investigator, Prof. Alison Cooley. The aim of the project is to make available, both to scholars and the wider public, the full collection of Latin inscriptions currently held by the Ashmolean Museum. In order to ensure the accessibility of this material, the decision was made to produce the catalogue in digital form only, which will be available as a free online database from 2016, and that this would be complemented by a programme of teaching resources for schools, blog, podcasts and new installations in the Ashmolean Museum. Subsequently, the AshLI team has expertise not only in 'pure' epigraphy, but in EpiDoc, digital imaging (notably Reflectance Transformation Imaging, for the enhancement of worn stones), blogging, podcasting, and visitor engagement.

The team has certainly found there to be no shortage of material. The last time the Ashmolean Museum conducted a critical inventory of its Latin inscriptions was 1763, with the publication of Richard Chandler's *Marmora Oxoniensia*. Unsurprisingly, a good deal has changed since the eighteenth-century, and the Museum has made a number of acquisitions. As we approach the final phase of the project, AshLI is now in a position to begin presenting our findings. At the first International EAGLE Conference (*Information Technologies for Epigraphy and Cultural Heritage*), held in Paris in 2014, we confidently announced that we had identified 300 Latin inscriptions on display and in storage at the Ashmolean Museum. As colleagues in other similar projects have discovered, further investigations have brought to light additional material, so that we currently have a total of 455 Latin inscriptions in the AshLI corpus.

The Nature of the Corpus

One of the challenges in working with this corpus is its great variety. It has not been selected on the basis of its geographical origins, support type, or date.

Instead, we have a ready-made corpus of inscriptions, defined by its physical presence in the Ashmolean Museum. And while it has very concrete boundaries, it does not have the internal coherence of a thematic corpus. The stones simply represent the particular whims of particular collectors, who each had different varied ideas about what was beautiful and interesting.

We have a huge variety of supports for our inscriptions which has created its own problems with EpiDoc encoding. We have monumental stones, pottery, glassware, a very fine collection of sling bullets, with polite and not so polite insults to the enemy on them, early Christian gold-glass (bases of vessels with gold leaf sandwiched between the layers of glass), gemstones, jewellery, metalware, and also appliqué metal letters, which have raised questions about categorization. Cataloguing these in EpiDoc has made us ask consistent questions about material that traditionally has not been treated in the same way. When, for example, AshLI came to study the Ashmolean sling bullets, we began by following the cataloguing traditions for sling bullets. But it transpired that these conventions required us to ask different questions of the material than, for example, the cataloguing conventions for stone monuments. Now that we are using EpiDoc, we are beginning to ask consistent and coherent questions, the same questions, for each different type of material that usually are not asked. It has been extremely interesting to see the result of this more consistent approach.

Applying EpiDoc to the AshLI Corpus

At the time of this conference, the AshLI project is at the start of its third and final year but, in terms of *encoding* the inscriptions into EpiDoc, only one year in. As a consequence, the questions that we have been asking of the material have evolved as we have got to grips with the diverse material in the collection. To date, we have encoded *c.* 300 of the 455 inscriptions in the Museum's collection. We began by encoding the more traditional, monumental stone inscriptions, and it has only been in the last 4-5 months that we have turned to the more unusual inscriptions.

The EAGLE meeting in Bari came at a very opportune time, since the questions that we were asked to consider about the physical support or about the execution of the technique are usually very much interrelated and as mentioned above, the AshLI project has an extremely wide variety of material supports. As a result, we have been thinking about what information we want to encode, and how we such tackle and try to standardise the encoding of inscriptions that traditionally have been dealt with in quite different ways, as regards textual editions and corpora.

The case studies, discussed below, present some of the key problems and issues that we have encountered through the process of encoding the editions. Currently, we have been working with the EpiDoc Example Stylesheets, and like other participants at the 6th EAGLE International Event, we have come up against the problem that the creation of new or unbounded values might have in the transformation and cross-walking of EpiDoc in HTML. The intention for the AshLI online database is to have specific Stylesheets designed by the Ashmolean Museum's IT Officer, Jonathan Moffett, whom we have been working with to create the project's website and searchable catalogue. Some of the below cases studies involve the proposal of new values, which will need to addressed in our Stylesheets.

Two categories of interest that relate to the encoding of the text:

1. Textual Transcriptions.

> We have a number of glyphs and symbols, some of which are well known and traditional: crosses, chi-rho, centurion mark, sestertius mark, leaf interpuncts, as well as some numerals, which are slightly unusual in their form (for example, ⊥, for the numeral 'L'), but can be dealt with using Unicode, and the Gaia mark, which will be discussed as a case study below.

> Also within the category of textual transcriptions, fall questions about the form and appearance of the characters. We have one interesting example that raises questions about how to encode new values concerning the appearances and relation of characters.

2. Layout of the Text.

> This includes the direction of the text and we have quite a few examples, which are in circles or semicircles, due to the nature of the support. Within this category we are also concerned with the execution of the writing and how that relates, in some instances quite intimately, to the physical support.

The Gaia mark

Our first case study does not, in certain respects, belong 'off the beaten track', given that our examples come from the traditional field of stone, monumental inscriptions, whose editions are highly standardised in the practice of epigraphy. Indeed, the Gaia mark, Ɔ, is a very well-known symbol in the traditional epigraphy practice. In terms of encoding the Gaia mark, it was very interesting to hear from Giulia Sarullo on the encoding that is being carried out for the *Inscriptiones Latinae Antiquissimae* project. Dr Sarullo noted the distinction between inverted characters in Archaic Latin inscriptions and in Classical Latin epigraphy: whereas in Archaic inscriptions these are just inverted characters with no significance, in

Classical Latin inscriptions such characters have additional meanings embedded in them. This means that such inverted characters must be encoded differently for Archaic Latin inscriptions and for Classical Latin inscriptions.

Currently, there is no specific information in the EpiDoc guidelines about how to treat the Gaia mark as a special character, although Dr Charlotte Tupman (King's College, London) has suggested to us that we use Unicode to achieve the letter-form. Moreover, an examination of different databases indicates that there is no consistent way of handling this value.

In its simplest interpretation the Gaia mark is an inverted character, which could be rendered thus:

<hi rend= 'inverted'>C</hi>

However, this encoding does little beyond indicate the letter-form, and in fact is of no use to us as it does not tell us the significant information that is embedded in that character. The inverted nature of the character signifies a special meaning. Should we then treat the Gaia mark as a symbol/gylph? In our initial treatment of the character we rendered it thus:

<g type='gaia'>U+0816</g>

Whereas, the Epigraphic Database Roma used the following value:

<g type='mulieris'>mulieris</g>

Whilst both these codes indicate the symbolic nature of the character, they fail to take into account what Quintilian has told us about the letter-form:

> *Nam et 'Gaius' C littera significatur, quae inversa mulierem declarat* (Quint. Inst. 1.28)
>
> 'Gaius' is indicated by the letter C, which, when inverted, signifies 'woman'.

'C' is traditionally treated as an abbreviation of *Gaius*, and encoded as such: <expan><abbr>C</abbr><ex>aius</ex><expan>. If the inverted character-form is viewed has having a similar function in relation to *mulieris*, then should it not be treated as an abbreviation as well? What we currently propose is to treat 'Ɔ' as a glyph within an abbreviation element:

<expan><abbr><am><gtype='gaia'>U+0186</g></am></abbr><ex>mulieris</ex></expan>

This allows us to express the letter-form and at the same time explain its significance in indicating, in abbreviated form, the word *mulieris*.

Form and appearance of the text

Within the collection we have quite standard characters that are required to be highlighted in EpiDoc such as ligatures, super-linear lines, super- and sub-scripts etc. One inscription, however, has character forms for which we have been unable to find a standard value within which to encode it. The monumental stone inscription, known as the Odda stone (Figure 1), dates to the 11th century AD, and in terms of chronology, stands very much in isolation from the rest of the collection. As Figure 1 makes clear, there are several letters within letters. These letters, all of which are vowels, are not ligatured or attached in any way, but rather they are set inside the preceding character. Such an example requires the creation of new values for the @rend to define these characters. Possible values would be 'inside' or 'inside-previous'. The creation of new values would, of course, cause problems in terms of the Stylesheets, because currently the example Stylesheets cannot handle new values in the rend attribute.

FIGURE 1. THE ODDA STONE (AN1896-1908 M.300), AN 11TH CENTURY INSCRIPTION ORIGINALLY FROM GLOUCESTERSHIRE, ENGLAND. AN UNUSUAL FEATURE OF THE INSCRIPTION IS THAT CERTAIN LETTERS ARE INSCRIBED WITHIN A PRECEEDING LETTER
(IMAGE: ASHMOLEAN LATIN INSCRIPTIONS PROJECT).

Execution techniques

The invitation to discuss the AshLI project's work at the 6th EAGLE International Event in Bari caused us to think about how we should describe the execution of the texts of our highly varied collection of inscriptions. We found the Silvia Evangelisti's descriptions of writing vocabularies on the EAGLE portal extremely useful for determining the correct value (@key=) for the execution of the text in relation to the different types of material supports we have.[1] For example, we originally thought to describe the execution of both brickstamps and *terra sigillata* as 'ex forma', given that they are both made from moulds, but Evangelisti's definitions shows that *ex forma* should only be applied to metal objects ('*Va utilizzato, quindi per quegli oggetti in cui l'epigrafe nello stampo per l'oggetto stesso e che sono solo di metallo*'), and that *signaculo* was the correct value to use for both these objects.

In determining the correct execution value for the objects in the Ashmolean collection, it was useful to categorise the techniques in terms of both hard and soft techniques, and whether the execution was achieved through the addition of material to the support, the subtraction of material from the support, or by modification of the material, such as creating an impression. Alongside these classifications, we also wanted to determine the nature of the material onto which the text was executed, as this will have an effect of the technique of execution if the material is hard or soft. We currently have the following three categories, each of which comprise a number of different execution values:

1. Additional/Hard techniques
   a. *litteris applicatis* (applied letters) e.g. gold glass, where the gold leaf is sandwiched between layers of glass.
   b. *pictura* (painted) e.g. Black Rhenish ware beaker with white barbotine decoration painted on the surface.
2. Subtractive/Hard techniques
   a. *scalpro* (inscribed) e.g. traditional, stone monumental epigraphy.
   b. *scariphatis* (stratched) e.g. graffito on pottery.
   c. *punctim* (punched) e.g. copper alloy votive *tabula ansata* with letters punched as dots onto the metal.
   d. *caelo* (engraved on metal) e.g. Silver? plaque of Jupiter, engraved.
3. Impression/Soft techniques
   a. *signaculo* (stampe) e.g. brickstamps and *terra sigillata* made from moulds, as well as the moulds themselves.
   b. *ex forma* (made from a mould) e.g. lead slingshot bullets and glass vessels, with text moulded on them.

---

[1] http://www.eagle-network.eu/voc/writing.html.

We have one final set of items, gemstones, which fall within the subtractive/hard technique category that we are still trying to determine the correct key value for. Whilst we might colloquially described gemstones as engraved, but we cannot use *caelo* (engraved) as this is limited to metal objects. It might be possible to apply one of the existing controlled vocabularies *terebro* (bored, perforated), however we are considering whether a new value might be applicable. Both Suetonius and Pliny the Elder use the verb *scalpo* to describe the engraving of signet rings,[2] which may recommend for the use of *scalpro* for gemstones.

Direction of the text

We have a number of inscriptions where the direction of the text is interesting. Several texts are in circles or semi-circles, which again is not something that can be handled in the current example Stylesheets. Quite a few of our inscriptions have retrograde characters, which are described using the direction of the text, rather that using an inverted character because we are not highlighting one character as inverted, but rather the entire text is retrograde and runs from right to left.

What is particularly interesting with our examples of retrograde texts is the reasons why the direction of the text runs from right to left. Objects with retrograde text in the Ashmolean collection are gemstones, moulds for *terra sigillata* and one brickstamp. The texts on the gemstones and the moulds are reversed because they are, in one respect, a tool within a process of production. The final text created from these objects – seals from gemstones, and *sigillata* from the moulds – will run from left to right, rather than right to left, and the text will no longer be retrograde. Our brickstamp (Figure 2) is unusual. All the other brickstamps in our collection have texts that run left to right (often in the circle), having been made from moulds, where the letters are retrograde. With this particular brickstamp, we might assume that the text on the mould ran left to right, and so the brickstamp, as the final product, has come out with the letters retrograde.

These examples of retrograde texts raise the question of the relationship between the execution of the text and the material support. When we are encoding the textual edition of an inscription we are concerned with what the letters say, whether there are abbreviations, any particular characters that need highlighting etc., but when we deal with the physical support we are concerned with the execution and the material. The final case study discussed below draws together these issues, and raises questions about what our aims are when encoding texts (Figure 3).

The object is a mid-first century AD, Flavian brickstamp, the product of two different brickyards ('Tonneian from the Viccianan brickyards'). The first line of

---

[2] Suet. Aug. 50; Pliny NH 37.4.

Figure 2. Top row, left to right: gemstone (AN1890.247) engraved with a crab and retrograde letters; brickstamp (ANTN1864) with retrograde letters; bottom: fragmentary terra sigillata mould (AN1889.14c) with retrograde letters (images: Ashmolean Latin Inscriptions Project).

the text runs in a semi-circle, and the second line runs left-right across the brick. The diplomatic and textual editions of the inscription are as follows:

TONNEI · DE FICILINIS / V[[ICCI]]ANIS

Tonnei(ana) · de fi⌈g⌉ilinis /V[[icci]]anis

<lb n='1' rend='semicircle'/> <expan><abbr>Tonnei</abbr><ex>ana</ex></expan> <g type='interpunct'/> de fi<choice><sic>c</sic><corr>g</corr></choice>ilinis

<lb n='2' rend='left-to-right'/> V<del rend='erasure'>icci</del>anis

The point of interest is the erasure in the second line,[3] which has been treated in the diplomatic and textual editions with the traditional Leiden convention, and

---

[3] The AshLI commentary for this brickstamp (AN1872.1527) states that 'it is not clear why the word Viccianis

Figure 3. First century AD brickstamp (AN1872.1527) with direction of text in semi-circle and left to right, and an erasure in the second line (image: Ashmolean Latin Inscriptions Project).

marked-up as such in XML. However, when we consider the physical object itself, we realised that the erasure was not produced on the support material that is to say on the brickstamp itself.

When we think about an erasure on an inscription, traditionally we expect to find a subtractive technique, a negative impression is left as something has been cut away.[4]

Such an example of a traditional erasure in epigraphy in the Ashmolean Collection is a votive altar from South Shields, in the North East of England, dedicated on behalf of Caracalla and his brother Geta (Figure 4).

Geta's name has been erased from the stone, with the use of a chisel to remove the stone bearing the text. In the case of our brickstamp however, the erasure stands proud from the surface, so that rather than being a negative impression of

---

has been partly erased, but it appears intact on other similar stamps'.

[4] In palaeography, however, an erasure may indeed be an additional technique.

FIGURE 4: VOTIVE ALTAR FROM SOUTH SHIELDS, ENGLAND (ANChandler 3.3), DEDICATED ON BEHALF OF CARACALLA AND GETA. GETA'S NAME HAS BEEN ERASED IN LINES 7-8 (IMAGE: ASHMOLEAN LATIN INSCRIPTIONS PROJECT).

the material surface, the erasure actually stands in relief. The reason for this is that the erasure was not created on the surface of the material support, but rather in the mould. Therefore, whilst the erasure exists in terms of the textual edition, it was not created as a part of the physical end product of the process.

This case study does not mean that we should not continue to encode such as text has having an erasure, as the characters are clearing missing from the textual edition, but it does prompt us to question what information we want to encode about the text, the material support and the execution technique, and how we see this aspects relating to one another.

Further information may be found on the AshLI blog, 'Reading, Writing, Romans', http://bit.ly/AshLI-blog *or by contacting the team by e-mail:* ashli@classics.ox.ac.uk. *The full digital corpus of the Ashmolean Latin Inscriptions will, from mid-2016, be available online at* http://latininscriptions.ashmus.ox.ac.uk.

Epigraphy out there

Pietro Liuzzo
Heidelberg University

This conference[1] has seen a unique meeting of scholars in Epigraphy, most of which have also initiated or led the most important databases of inscriptions available online. Almost all the pioneers of Digital Epigraphy were in Bari, together with Carlo Carletti, the creator of the Epigraphic Database Bari[2] and Silvia Orlandi, Coordinator of the EAGLE project,[3] whose words I'd like to borrow to begin these conclusive remarks of the conference:

'EAGLE is a good example of what Europe can be'.

EAGLE is indeed a growing network of highly skilled engineers and humanists cooperating positively towards a common goal. As a late comer who has had the honor to serve this cause in the last three years only, I believe the dreams of those setting up the first databases of inscriptions ten, twenty or even thirty or forty years ago, can be seen going fast forward in this conference.[4] The ideas and motivations behind the efforts put in collecting and documenting inscriptions have remained virtually unchanged and probably exactly for that reason epigraphic databases have kept up with times and got wiser about tools and methodologies, including networking and a good interaction with the European context.[5] From this conference we start to see the results of all the work carried out during the EAGLE project but also during the last decades. We see also quite clearly the work ahead of us for the next years at least, with a special twist towards the boundaries of the discipline, i.e. those areas of interest which are more challenging the definitions (Panciera 2012), ground concepts and methodology, thus feeding more the progress of theoretic research.

Let me try to summarize what we have been speaking about during this conference 'Epigraphy off the beaten track', in Bari, at the end of September 2015, so that the scope of it might become evident. Geographically we have seen inscriptions from Yemen to the United Kingdom. Chronologically we have covered from VII century BC to XV century AD more or less. We have spoken about Museum

---

[1] This text reproduces without substantial changes the speech given on September 25th 2015 in Bari, as a Conclusion to the conference.
[2] www.edb.uniba.it
[3] www.eagle-network.eu
[4] Feraudi-Gruénais (2010), Terras (2010). See also Rocco (2016) for an example based on EDB.
[5] For a history of the changes occurred in Epigraphy see Bodel (2012).

collections, editions and corpora, databases, false and original inscriptions, cities, provinces, several ancient languages and scripts, above and under the surface of the world's whereabouts. That was quite an impressive and widely diverse scope, but with a strong connection and unity among all the presentations, linked by a special trait of peculiarity, of exception from the mainstream.[6] Is then all or most epigraphy 'off the beaten track'? We have jumped from exceptions to difficulties and rarities with stimulating discussions. We have seen many problems and some solutions, all off which seem to hint to the fact that there is a lot still to do for our inscribed monuments and the people we want to reach and make interested in them.

There is also, and it could be gauged during this conference, an aim which has significantly grown in importance, keeping pace with what the new methodologies could offer. It was not possible to offer to a wider public to learn about inscriptions in the XIX century and for the almost all the XX century it was necessary to access a library to learn that epigraphy existed. But now also epigraphy can become accessible to a much larger number of people and during these few days it seemed clear that no researcher wants to miss this opportunity to fulfill such mission towards society. The challenge is than to tell, but not to simplify, what is actually interesting in an inscription also to those who have chosen not to study or to study something else and have little knowledge of ancient history and epigraphy.

We might not be able to provide answers even if, with databases, we can return results to a query with a certain degree of certainty and precision. Nevertheless we can satisfy some curiosity, ours first and that of other scholars as well as of the people just out there.[7] Scholars in epigraphy have marked a huge step to free themselves from their predecessors and want people to 'walk out and be surprised about inscriptions', to quote again the introductory remarks of the conference: we want to bring the texts and the monuments back where they belonged, out of the ivory towers of libraries and under the eyes of people, in the public for citizens and not citizens, a task served very well by the Web. Computer Engineers, Digital Humanists and Digital Librarians, are pulling even further and call researchers in epigraphy to renew the methodologies once more, and again to the benefit of specialists and non specialists, by making resources linked, accessible, machine actionable and reusable.[8]

Given these general observations, I would like to make three points more in details, summarizing suggestions which were discussed during these two days

---

[6] See the contributions in Bodard-Mahony 2010. A list of projects, giving the idea of the diversity, can be found on digital classicist wiki: https://wiki.digitalclassicist.org/Category:Epigraphy
[7] A mission which the EAGLE portal, Storytelling application and Virtual Exhibition took on board but which is wonderfully carried out by initiatives as the Blog of the Ashmolean Museum 'Reading, Writing, Romans' http://www.ashmolean.org/ashwpress/latininscriptions/ .
[8] Among many others, see Hyvönen 2012, Heath- Bizer 2011.

of wonderfully organized event. One point is about the problems and solutions for editing epigraphic texts which have emerged and it includes a digression on vocabularies; the second is about the general landscape of epigraphy and some ideas for the future which in these last months emerged; the last conclusive point I would like to make is about the so called 'problem' of sustainability.

Editing epigraphic texts

One noticeable fact during this conference is that no one failed to mention EpiDoc.[9] Most projects, whichever their aim is, use it or want to use it, and so does EAGLE as an aggregator.[10] Everyone nevertheless seems to use EpiDoc in different ways, confronting themselves with it from different angles. Among the epigraphies at the outskirts of mainstream Greco-Roman epigraphy, this XML standard seems to be the track most people follow, but in diverse ways. Let me then spend a word on it, related to the issues highlighted during the conference.

EpiDoc has gently become a standard for its usability and the work constantly carried on to maintain it and to build tools to make its adoption easier day after day. There are nevertheless still some clashes between the intention of those who maintain EpiDoc and the users, and this does not surprise off course. Once learned the practical 'how' of encoding, results might be quickly convincing and encouraging, but I believe there is still a strong need to pause on the theoretical background in order to go from enthusiasm to conscious persuasion.

Tom Elliott (2014: 82), the creator of EpiDoc, defines EpiDoc very clearly when he says

> 'EpiDoc methodology, uses XML to encode and manipulate the underlying semantics of the epigraphic editorial process.'

Each word in this definition is pondered and needs to be understood to avoid expecting from EpiDoc to be something it is not, like a very sophisticated database or software for inscriptions from which one can get certain functionalities out of the box. Once embraced encoding as a methodology of work and XML as the preferred way to encode and TEI as the more adequate XML schema, the questions we can ask 'to EpiDoc' are the same we ask when we prepare a printed edition, they are connected to the editorial process, not to database structures, software, interfaces or archives: what is relevant? what do I want to note and describe in this document?

---

[9] EpiDoc is the name of a specialization of the Text Encoding Initiative (TEI), for ancient documents, it consists mainly of a schema to validate XML descriptions, a set of sample XSLT and Guidelines. http://epidoc.sourceforge.net/, Elliott et. al. 2007-2015.
[10] Rivero Ruiz et. al. 2015, Mannocci et. al. 2014.

Encoding goes deep into the semantics, it does not stop at data entry in a very well structured frame. Sometimes we have heard questions of description like 'where do I put this kind of information?', e.g. the description of the layout of the text. Sometimes we have heard questions of prescriptiveness, 'which element should I use for this specific case? How should I structure my data?'. I believe a general answer can be found in this statement from the Columbia Guide to Digital Publishing, in a chapter significantly entitled *TEI: a wealth of options*.[11]

> 'The fundamental thing to understand about TEI is that it is essentially *descriptive* rather than *prescriptive*. It reflects the needs of its originators to describe virtually any document - a Novel, a seventeenth-century economics treatise, a fragment of a medieval manuscript, a poem, a scene from a play - in a way that is not only manageable by the computer but useful to the scholar. It is not concerned, to the extent ISO 12083 is, with how a publication *ought* to be structured; its mission is to give scholars of any kind of document a way to describe how it *is* structured.' (Kasdorf 2003: 111)

Neither the Epigrapher has an answer, neither the engineer: the first would rather prefer a field in a *scheda* to fill according to a very specific methodology (a prescriptive approach), the second faces that as a 'domain specific' question and starts to be concerned when a valid dataset has already been prepared. There is clearly a missing set of distinct skills and specific expertise, those of a Digital Epigraphist / Classicist, who understands and cares about what XML does, and what it is for, and thus questions, e.g. the potential in between the specific domain and the technologies.[12] An engineer and an historian do not do the trick even if they are together in the same room or work for the same project.[13]

The projects presented during this conference using EpiDoc have demonstrated very well how much more potential there is in an encoded text compared to a databases, but since the 'Hows' and 'Whys' remain in the shade of the results we find ourselves assuming that it is enough to learn how to encode to find a solution to all problems. Although EpiDoc is a key and provides many and very useful tools it cannot solve problems alone, it offers more potential in generating relevant problems and a methodology of work which might facilitate multiple possible solutions. This is because somehow, as a methodology, encoding takes a step back from the technological newness of databases and provides standards and tools to carry out in a better way the same editorial process which is traditionally carried out by researchers.

---

[11] For the Text Encoding Initiative, see http://www.tei-c.org/index.xml
[12] Terras (2010: 172-174 and 177) explores the definition of the Digital Classicist.
[13] See Spiro 2012 for a brief overview of the debate about defining Digital Humanities.

One major difference and improvement which the semantic web can definitely do compared to traditional methodologies to encode a text[14] is that it can do even better magic with input from many problems, exceptions, peculiarities. Anyone can put a feature request in the EpiDoc website for each of the problems encountered and these will be addressed; anyone can share to the trunk repository the code developed for his own projects. Traditional methodologies and software on the other side call for passive learning and application, or even require to adapt the content to the software or the editorial rules imposed by the editors. Such methods might get just some erudite criticism before being challenged by a new software. EpiDoc encoding of ancient documents is open and anyone who has the will to do so can get involved in the mailing lists and blogs, ask there the questions, accept discussion and feel any way free to take different decisions, encode only something etc. and if the file is valid, it is already 'fine'.

Encoding ancient documents unity is achieved together with freedom and cooperation, not with rules and prescriptions to be imposed. In a database there are fields to be filled, there is no freedom out of that tabular structure. With XML we can almost forget about having a field for the information we want to enter and we can write what we want, and tag (or not) in a quite articulated way any information we identify as useful in the text we are editing, according to what is the plan we have for that information, what we would like to do with it. In most cases to describe a specific feature a line of description would be a better prescription and recommendation than a specific structured field into which to force the information. The layout of the text is a good example of this.

It is than a very good sign of change which we can observe from this conference, how the traditional, exegetical and methodological questions are addressed to EpiDoc. Epigraphic scholarship accepted to be challenged, and is changing with it (Parry 2010). This requires sometime also to understand that a new question can be asked or that a certain concern belongs to a distinct area of preoccupation, e.g. editorial decisions cannot be solved by a standard for encoding ancient texts, although this can help a lot if used wisely. In some cases this means some problems are just not there any more and all we need to do is exercise judgement and get going with the research and the description of our document.

This separation of concerns is in itself a big challenge. When we say 'what to do with your markup is a different set of questions', for example, teaching summer schools about XML and EpiDoc, we think this is a purely scientific discrimination which can be taken for granted to be good. I believe that the world of WYSIWYG

---

[14] 'The Epigrapher is an Encoder' as Bodard clearly explains in the teaching materials of the EpiDoc Summer Schools (wiki.digitalclassicist.org/EpiDoc_Summer_School). Bodard 2010.

software has given a very strong blow to that while the Semantic Web holds onto that very strongly, recognizing and exploiting the value in each distinct concern.[15] The semantic web is a more traditional method of research than writing the edition of an ancient document in a text editor, because it is strictly concerned with the study and description of a document and simply offers a different methodology. A corpus of inscriptions or a book put together directly as we want it at the end jumps ahead of these scientific separations of concerns, supporting the speed in production of results to the detriment of the analytical phase.

A further separated concern is 'what you want to be able to do with your data', and this contains a set of new questions and possibilities, which in a print only project would have not even touched the mind of the author, whose work, once printed in a book, finished. This methodology then opens a series of questions: what do I do with my data? what readers and users do with it? what other authors and editors could do with it? And this brings up again new scientifically separated concerns in a fruitful and thoughts provoking process.

We can also mention the concern for interoperability, so 'how do I do it so that it is useful to others'. This is a question which searches for prescriptions among freedom and forgets about the inherent values of the methodology and the standards it uses. Interoperability will always require some work, but the experience of EAGLE demonstrate that in comparison the aggregation of whatever EpiDoc (i.e. XML encoded) corpus of inscriptions requires hundreds times less time and effort than any other interoperability attempt within the domain.

The other is the problem of maintenance. A published book meant the end of a given research project. Updates would just end up in a new project of update to that volume, taking again the form of a volume. The data produced in a machine and software independent way as XML, is dynamic, can be and needs to be continuously updated. It is an entirely new way of doing research. One could claim the only real aim of a researcher studying ancient documents should be to produce such data, and that others should instead take care of how it is displayed and printed.

This conference has seen these changes at a stage at which they are getting well rooted in the mind of scholars and it is indeed encouraging although it should not make us lower the guard and forget about the principles and the definitions. To carry on steadily we shall build on, but keep up with the basics. As in a healthy run, we do not need to rush neither to start too fast, which does not help on the middle and long term.

---

[15] See the Stack of expressive power Berners-Lee 2007, also in Bodel 2012.

Vocabularies

Another major question is that of definitions of terms. What is that? an altar? a statue base? can we say that it is simply a stone, or we have to be more accurate because we can be? how to define something if the value is not in my dropdown list? In the database world we adapted and used the closest match possible. In the semantic web era we enrich the resources to be able to say what we want to say to the best of our knowledge (Liuzzo et al. 2014: 21; 2015: 23), without letting the structure rule us, but having the machine to work for our research aims, to quote once more a key teaching of Gabriel Bodard's EpiDoc Workshops.

There are scientific problems which some new finds might clarify, but no technology will be able to solve, neither recognizing images or having tools to explore the texture of a 3D model, although these could greatly help archeologists in their studies. Nevertheless, new approaches have been developed and are offered, so that, from the standpoint of a machine-actionable, encoded ancient document, one could express much more than simply stating what something is. Very often the same 'Thing' is called in very different ways,[16] and there is no need to involve Cratylus to be aware of this, but while in a text or in an utterance that choice is unavoidable, and thus leads to the need of specific clarification, in the Web this can be safely and securely abandoned as a concern in such form, at least at the encoding level (it might certainly be a point at display level). One Thing can have as many names as we have given to it as people, and can be called whatever way. We'll just make sure to align the name to the Thing it calls for, trying not to exaggerate the number of Things and remain reasonable to the aims of our projects, once more prioritizing the research question instead of the display or the results. Names and Things both have identifiers in the Web of Things and we can give a number or an arbitrary sequence of letter to any of those, to allow a fuller description. In this way, serving a need of precision and quality, we also provide ways to extend the contents reach and richness. It's a win-win-win-etc. situation.

When we enter a link to Things, Names and definitions, we actually perform the very same job of our predecessors, the ancient scholars and erudite copyists who added *scholia* to manuscripts.[17] Some wise monk had left margins, and some wiser reader had filled them up with notes, explanations, definitions, because man's curiosity and thirst for knowledge claim always more space. The space we are given by the Web enables those notes to be more numerous, deeper and more precise and we have been only sorry till recent time, not to be able to add two or more links on a word.[18] Try to click *Sepulcralis* on an EDB record with that

---

[16] Keller 2011, https://www.w3.org/WoT/
[17] The description and methodology of the Homer Multitext Project make this in a way self-evidents (http://www.homermultitext.org/about.html).
[18] This is theoretically something which has been overcome by networks of information and data architecture of the semantic web of things, as Pelagios and SNAP:DRNG.

inscription type, and you will find out translations, definitions, further examples of that type, as well as other inscriptions with a connection to that specific Thing. It certainly requires some more time for building those Vocabularies nicely and to make those connections live, but the worth of it is quite clear, as it is the research potential. I would like also to add that the curation of such lists is no new job as well, if we think of some types of inscriptions such as lists of priests and Ephebs, and many other types of lists.

Such resources once fully displayed in a browser might turn out to be very fragile indeed and can become the apotheosis of distraction for readers. Nevertheless we are not articulating thoughts or asking the machine to describe our documents and tell us already the answers to our research questions. A digital linked edition, and the vocabularies it refers to are made to open paths for the articulation of ideas, a natural need of research. We are feeding immediate curiosity and offering connections which will need to be studied. We are actually bringing to the surface possible questions and connections, not just providing a static resource for reference. A linked data edition is a research-generating-product, not just a product of research. Building a digital edition serves the people who will look at those links to Things and ask themselves: why is there a link between these two objects?

Sure enough when databases get too big or too complex, nevermind the wiseness of the structure and architecture, they can fail to serve their primary function of access to data. Try to find a simple flower in Wikidata. It's hard job and might make one think: then what's the use of all this? There is a *momentum* to be found between the aspiration to communicate and the tendency to hide Knowledge, as Schopenauer would say, also in the Web of Things. But is a work for all us to do, at least in our own discipline. I don't think we'll ever really call it https://www.wikidata.org/wiki/Q886167, so there is nothing to fear, but perhaps we'll be able to say things which are comprehensible to more people, because they are translated, explained, connected and contextualized.

Linked Open Data, with its Things, Names, connections and Vocabularies is somehow also more rooted in traditional scholarship than results-only oriented technologies.

The landscape of digital epigraphy

> 'Databases were created, like their older cousins for literary and papyrological texts, with search and discovery in mind. It was generally assumed by their creators that for any item of interest identified through a database the user would then follow up by consulting the original publications in order to get access to the full apparatus, commentary, analysis, and so forth.

> This assumption also assuaged the concerns of many in early days that intellectual property rights might be trampled by wholesale digitization of print resources.' (Elliott 2014: 80)

This statement should be kept in mind when considering how much more we work today with digital resources and how much we take for granted that they should be there. It is easy today to hear 'you can find everything online!' but this is clearly untrue to anyone who has worked to digitize contents. Such conception blinds a generation of academics and students, not to speak of the general public, who assumes this as a fact and supports general statements on the basis of online information. Non Digital Academics think there is no need to digitize more, cause somebody else does it or has done it all already (not clear who); Students instead might think they have completed their research because they have searched some database online.[19]

Today ancient Greek and Latin inscriptions online are really very numerous (see image below), but to think they are all there in any or among all the different databases is simply wrong. Nevertheless, since the stage is such why we all struggle to enter the same one in three different databases is quite obscure and rather a different question from valuing diversity. Collaborating to this collection of inscribed documents now that it can be unified and commonly developed is understandably much better for everyone, without any need to compare costs and benefits, has the first have been met already and the second are numerous and self-evident to anyone who does not really think to have ownership of a territory for inscription's hunting.

Let's look at this image from Europeana Strategy 2020, a document which is not simply outlining the future of the major common digital resource for Europe, but also giving a valuable overview on what is going on, thus helping everyone to understand where to head next.[20] If we compare the total of digitized Cultural Heritage Objects with digitized inscriptions, it looks like are doing really well, at least for Greek and Roman epigraphy.[21] Less nicely if we look at how much stuff is actually reusable in a nice and open format. Worst if you glance at the useless duplication of work and at the areas not properly covered by anyone, which are not just the endangered areas of the Near East.

---

[19] On the users of digital epigraphy see Löser 2014 and Varga 2014.
[20] http://strategy2020.europeana.eu/
[21] Data comes from EAGLE (http://www.eagle-network.eu/) and IDEs (http://ides.io/) and has been evaluated with experts. It should although not be taken as precise, as there is no mean to evaluate the total number of inscriptions, at least until we all will work digitally in a machine actionable standardized form.

Figure 1. Digitized Cultural Heritage in Europe (from http://strategy2020.europeana.eu by Elco van Staveneren)

Europeana has been a very nice step for epigraphic databases to change mindset (and also prepare all needed assets) from that of the searchable database to that of the linked and collaborative digital edition. We are only a step away from taking epigraphy out of the deep and dark web and make it surface. But most of you know the threats as well as the benefits. At some points we risked over a metadata mapping question, not to be able to publish the texts of the inscriptions because they basically did not feet a model (Liuzzo 2015).

Some things we now have are:

- data conversion tools for an interoperable export developed and used by EAGLE for several projects;
- data entry services as SoSOL for papyri.info or the one which the colleagues of the DASI project has shown us and the Leiden+ Javascript library prepared by Attic Inscriptions Online;
- numerous tailored ontologies and schemas for different types of contents and relations;
- guidelines for anything, with FAQ support, mailing lists, etc.;
- cookbooks for places and personal names;

- common controlled vocabularies;
- identified places and toponyms;
- ways to clearly share the images we have;
- aggregators and content checkers;
- peer review systems tested and validated (always SoSOL);
- federated searches, ontology based searches and multiple analytical tools to be simply plugged in;

Just to mention some. So I believe the time is mature to take the next step towards a real integrated epigraphic browser and editor. That is not a work of one day, although, because at the time I am writing this conclusions, we don't have, which hasn't been mentioned in the last days

- an open access database for Greek inscriptions;
- geolocation of Greek inscriptions (beside the LSAG ones. (static));
- vocabularies for Greek inscriptions, although the AXON project has aligned its controlled vocabularies to the EAGLE Vocabularies;
- the possibility to search across types of documents and sources (coins, inscriptions, papyri, literary sources), because although there are linked data vocabularies they are not implemented;
- open access data input for all records with a suitable board of editors instead of the local editorial boards;
- interoperability and integration of resources;
- translations of the documents;
- openly accessible images available via international protocols;
- workflow coordination;
- workforce and effort maximization via community work;
- etc.

But we are in a position where we could do most of these things.

We have done something for the last 30 years, and we need to get ready for the next 20 at least: just searching is not anymore what we can and want to offer, neither what people look for. If they find related contents in Amazon, why shouldn't they find related content about Ancient Documents, which are so much more important? Users also want to browse and navigate the resources, as much as the crawlers of the Internet Archive would like web pages and resources rather than hidden databases. There is also a large cohort of people who would like to directly contribute to the resources they use.

I believe that people need to be able to look at an epigraphic database or at an aggregator (EAGLE, Europeana, etc.) first, whichever of the many available, and start from there as the authoritative source of access further information and carry on with their research work. Ideally all these would use the same source files. This requires in the future of epigraphic databases a toughened network of integrated resources.

What I would like to imagine, after this conference, for the future of Epigraphy is one source edition in XML for one inscription, which becomes part of an online database days after being found (why not hours?) through a data entry app used on field research and connected to the relevant knowledge bases. This record in XML, once improved and reviewed, becomes a comprehensive digital publication, months after (certainly not years!), gathering input from the community of interested users, when the research has been carried out or directly at the beginning if the archeologist recognizes he might benefit from some expert work and collaboration. Any new idea on each given document becomes an update for the source file of that text again and again, reproducing the genetic bibliography of an edition.

What can be seen from this meeting, is that in the very near future there will be a community who works around a common effort, following and improving on the example of other well established initiatives and enhancing the benefits of the interaction with the ways of doing things of grown up communities like Wikimedia.

In the near future those who evaluate our work to decide what will be our future, will need to ask 'where are your contributions to digital projects? Where are your edits to EAGLE, your new Wikipedia pages, items etc.?' in order to ask 'what is the impact of your research' and perhaps we should give some thoughts at how to use DOIs to identify each approved contribution so that it can be quoted exactly as a normal journal contribution, more or less as Pleiades already does. Each inscription would have then not just a revision history, but a genetic bibliography of publications.

> Mario Rossi, CIL, X 123456, in EAGLE 27/1/2016 (reviewed by Francois Verdin and John Smith), doi:99.9999/123456/2

> Gino Bianchi, CIL, X 123456, in EAGLE 28/9/2015 (reviewed by Fritz Grun and Xiao Chan), doi:99.9999/123456/1

This is a bibliographic annotation[22] where the DOI could simply resolve to the precise version of the resource and could be produced directly with bibliographic data.

---

[22] Aligned to MODs XML, FRBRoo or to other simple interchange standards of bibliographic information as the Zotero RDF to facilitate translations and mappings.

Submitting an edit or a change[23] would then be a simple way to submit a paper about a proposed change to the text, translation or any other data entity.

The description of the edit proposed will be the text explaining the proposed new reading and will not just be a text field, but might include the potential of editorial tools as the EAGLE Storytelling application,[24] to bring in content from online authoritative sources to support the statement, as well as functionalities to ease the argumentation process. Once accepted the resource would be updated and a bibliographical annotation generated registering the publication. This same dataset used to produce the change could also be taken and printed out in its final version if one wished for example to print this journal entry or a summary list of new readings of published texts.

The time in which we had to decide between a database and an edition looks like it is gone and we have decided all, independently as far as can be said by this conference, for the latter. The digital edition which we can make of these texts in XML can in fact be very simply, but much more powerfully, used as a database: the benefits are enormously greater than the effort required. Embracing the progress being made the presenters at this conference I believe demonstrated that the time is ripe for further steps. A revolution has already happened, even more than it was last year, at the meeting in Paris where this started to become really tangible and visible (Orlandi et al. 2014).

Sustainability and Conclusions

Using XML, does not mean you want to do a website, many books commercialized just as printed are actually produced in XML. It is a fact that we have seen many website and online databases during this conference because of the advantages this kind of medium has over print material, but let's keep to those for the last consideration. At the Europeana Annual General Meeting in 2014, a guest speaker from the Internet Archive, nicely stressed a point we tend to forget, although we worry about it all time: web-sites die. We have all experienced website disappearing,[25] if not that a certain look of a website was replaced by a new one, and certainly we have complained about links not working anymore for the many reason a link can stop working (Elliott 2014: 79). On the contrary it is harder that a source file, if it has been shared in the appropriate places and communities is going to disappear.

---

[23] Which is now possible thanks to the SoSOL and its Perseids development, see Baumann 2013.
[24] http://www.eagle-network.eu/stories/ Developed as a Wordpress Plug-in the EAGLE Storytelling app is directly connected with EAGLE, Europeana, Wikipedia, Arachne and many other resources.
[25] The best data about the lifespan of a webpage is given by the Internet Archive at 77 days only. https://archive.org/about/faqs.php

XML alone, even with a nice infrastructure and a community, is not an answer, but digitally is really the best thing we can do, and even better if we can print it, share it, copy it, reuse it, transform it, aggregate it, so that, exactly as a good quality medieval manuscript, it functions as an archetype and gets copied many times rising the chances of survival of its contents.

Making data openly accessible and sharing it is a big part of the answer. The more people use data and care about it, the better are the chances that the research work survives to the next generation. Holding on the data does not help and is in fact dangerous: we have all heard of years and years of work going lost in 'old' computers. Another best practice is web archiving awareness: editions of texts surfaced to the web, and not hidden in the 'deep web' of databases can be crawled by projects as the Internet Archive,[26] or National Web Archives[27] and thus preserved for a bit longer.

Gregory Crane said at the DHAnt Conference in Grenoble few weeks before this conference that Classics are a uniquely universal subject. So is the Semantic Web. Both the Web and Classics are universal despite the language differences and the internal diversity, thus they get well together. This has been certainly confirmed by this conference. Epigraphy, in the shape of Digital Epigraphy, is taking an epochal step along a path which goes towards research resources we have been only dreaming of for decades. It has been an honor to be part of this conference and to see this change from within the EAGLE project.

Bibliography

Baumann, R. 2013. The Son of Suda On-Line. In S. Mahony and S. Dunn (eds.), *The Digital Classicist*: 91-106. London, The Institute of Classical Studies University of London.

Berners-Lee T., 2007. Introduction to the Semantic Web, slideshow. Decentralized Information Group. MIT Computer Science and Artificial Intelligence Laboratory. http://dig.csail.mit.edu/2007/Talks/0108-sw-tbl/#(1)

Bodel, J. 2012. Latin Epigraphy and the IT revolution. In J. Davies and J. Wilkes (eds.), *Epigraphy and the Historical Sciences*: 275-296. Oxford, Oxford University Press.

Bodard, G. and Mahony, S. (eds.) 2010. Digital research in the study of classical antiquity. Farnham-Burlington, Ashgate.

---

[26] https://archive.org/index.php, https://en.wikipedia.org/wiki/Internet_Archive, https://en.wikipedia.org/wiki/Wayback_Machine
[27] https://en.wikipedia.org/wiki/List_of_Web_archiving_initiatives

Bodard, G., 2009. EpiDoc: Epigraphic documents in XML for publication and interchange. In F. Feraudi-Gruenais (ed.), *Latin on Stone: Epigraphic Research and Electronic Archives*: 1–17. Lanham, Lexington Books.

Cayless, H., Roueché, C., Elliott, T. and Bodard, G. 2009. Epigraphy in 2017. In G. Crane and M. Terras (eds.), *Changing the Center of Gravity: Transforming Classical Studies Through Cyberinfrastructure*: 3.1 http://www.digitalhumanities.org/dhq/vol/3/1/000030/000030.html

Elliott, T., Bodard, G., Milonas, E., Stoyanova, S., Tupman, C. and Vanderbilt, S. 2007. EpiDoc Guidelines: Ancient documents in TEI XML. http://www.stoa.org/epidoc/gl/latest/.

Elliott, T. 2014. Epigraphy and Digital Resources. In C. Bruun and J. Edmondson (eds.), *The Oxford Handbook of Roman Epigraphy*: 78–85. Oxford, Oxford University Press.

Feraudi-Gruenais, F. (ed.), *Latin on Stone: Epigraphic Research and Electronic Archives*. Lanham, Lexington Books.

Heath, T. and Bizer, C. 2011. Linked Data: Evolving the Web into a Global Data Space. http://www.morganclaypool.com/doi/abs/10.2200/S00334ED1V01Y201102WBE00

Hyvönen, E. 2012. Publishing and Using Cultural Heritage Linked Data on the Semantic Web. *Synthesis Lectures on Semantic Web: Theory and Technology*: 2.1 http://www.morganclaypool.com/doi/pdf/10.2200/S00452ED1V01Y201210WBE003

Kasdorf, W. E. 2003. The Columbia Guide to Digital Publishing. New York, Columbia University Press.

Keller, M.A. 2011. Linked Data: A Way Out of the Information Chaos and toward the Semantic Web. *EDUCAUSE Review* 46.4 http://er.educause.edu/articles/2011/7/linked-data-a-way-out-of-the-information-chaos-and-toward-the-semantic-web

Liuzzo, P. M., Fasolini, D. and Rocco, A. 2015. Content Harmonisation guidelines, including GIS and terminologies. Second Release. http://www.eagle-network.eu/wp-content/uploads/2013/06/EAGLE_D2.2.2_Content-harmonisation-guidelines-including-GIS-and-terminologies-Second-Release.pdf

Liuzzo, P. M., Verreth, H. and Evangelisti, S., 2014. Content Harmonisation guidelines, including GIS and terminologies. First Release. http://www.eagle-network.eu/wp-content/uploads/2013/06/EAGLE_D2.2.1_Content-harmonisation-guidelines-including-GIS-and-terminologies.pdf

Liuzzo, P. M. 2015. EAGLE and EUROPEANA. Architecture Problems for Aggregation and Harmonization. In *Proceedings of the Symposium on Cultural Heritage Markup. Balisage Series on Markup Technologies*: 16.1 http://www.balisage.net/Proceedings/vol16/html/Liuzzo01/BalisageVol16-Liuzzo01.html

Löser, L. 2014. Meeting the Needs of Today's Audiences of Epigraphy with Digital Editions. In S. Orlandi, R. Santucci, V. Casarosa and P. M. Liuzzo (eds.), *Information Technologies for Epigraphy and Cultural Heritage. Proceedings of the First EAGLE International Conference*: 239–250. Roma, Sapienza Università Editrice.

Mannocci, A., Casarosa, V., Manghi, P. and Zoppi, F., 2014. The Europeana network of ancient Greek and Latin epigraphy data infrastructure. In S. Closs, R. Studer, E. Garoufallou and M.-A. Sicilia, *Metadata and Semantics Research. Proceedings of the 8th Research Conference, MTSR 2014 (Karlsruhe, November 27-29, 2014)*: 286–300. New York, Springer International Publishing. doi:10.1007/978-3-319-13674-5_27

Orlandi, S., Santucci, R., Casarosa and Liuzzo, P. M. (eds.), 2014. Information technologies for epigraphy and cultural heritage. Proceedings of the first EAGLE international conference. Roma, Sapienza Università Editrice.

Panciera, S., 2012. What Is an Inscription? Problems of Definition and Identity of an Historical Source. *Zeitschrift für Papyrologie und Epigraphik* 183: 1–10.

Parry, D. 2010. Be Online or Be Irrelevant. *AcademHack*: January 11, 2010. http://academhack.outsidethetext.com/home/2010/be-online-or-be-irrelevant/.

Rivero Ruiz, E., Manghi, P., Mannocci, A., Sicilia, M.-A., Gomez Pantoja, J., Rubiro Fuentes, J. and Zoppi, F., 2015. EAGLE metadata model specification. Second Release. http://www.eagle-network.eu/wp-content/uploads/2013/06/EAGLE_D3.1_EAGLE-metadata-model-specification_v1.1.pdf

Rocco, A. 2016. EDB 2.0. How Eagle Europeana project improved the Epigraphic Database Bari. In S. Orlandi, R. Santucci, F. Mambrini and P. M. Liuzzo (eds.), *Digital and Traditional Epigraphy in Context. Proceedings of the Second EAGLE International Conference (Rome, 27-29 January 2016)*: 73-90. Roma, Sapienza Università Editrice.

Spiro, L. 2012. 'This Is Why We Fight': Defining the Values of the Digital Humanities. In M. K. Gold (ed.), *Debates in the Digital Humanities*: 16-34. Minneapolis, University of Minnesota Press.

Terras, M. 2010. The Digital Classicist: disciplinary focus and interdisciplinary vision. In G. Bodard and S. Mahony (eds.), *Digital research in the study of classical antiquity*: 171–189. Farnham-Burlington, Ashgate.

Varga, R., 2014. (Digital) epigraphy as viewed by Romanian Archaeology/Classics Students. In S. Orlandi, R. Santucci, V. Casarosa and P. M. Liuzzo (eds.), *Information Technologies for Epigraphy and Cultural Heritage. Proceedings of the First EAGLE International Conference (Paris, 29-30 September – 1 October 2015)*: 233-238. Roma, Sapienza Università Editrice.